# 1 Introduction

In many decisions under uncertainty, individuals base their choices on what they learn from observing the choices of others as well as noisy private information, which can lead to herding behavior.[1] However, herding may be discouraged if costs are incurred when an individual follows the action of too many others. For example, observing people on their way to a restaurant or a rival firm opening a new location provides information about the relative quality of their chosen alternative but also increases the likelihood that one who follows them will be penalized because the location has already reached capacity. Though such decisions have received little attention in the literature,[2] they create a rich environment for exploring broader questions about herding behavior. In this paper, I develop a model of herding with capacity constraints called the Restaurant Game and study play of this game in a lab experiment. The results provide new insights on the extent to which the common bias in herding behavior can be explained by Level-$k$ thinking and other factors such as strategic uncertainty and cognitive ability.

A common observation in herding experiments is that subjects rely more on their private information and less on social learning than predicted by the risk-neutral Bayesian Nash equilibrium (see Hung and Plott (2001), Noth and Weber (2003), Celen and Kariv (2004a, 2005), Goeree et al. (2007), Weizsacker (2010) and March et al. (2012)).[3] A possible explanation for this phenomenon is provided by Level-$k$ thinking, a model of bounded rationality in which individuals act under inconsistent beliefs about the rationality of others (see Stahl and Wilson (1994), Nagel (1995), Camerer et al. (2004) and Crawford and Iriberri (2007)). According to this model, individuals overweight private information because they fail to make inferences about unseen information from

---

[1]See Banerjee (1992), Bikhchandani et al. (1992) for seminal work on this idea.

[2]The most closely related theoretical work is the Veeraraghavan and Debo (2008) study of strategic location of services with uncertain quality and waiting costs to consumers. Eyster and Rabin (2010) discuss a variant of their model of naive herding which includes small negative payoff externalities of choosing the same as others. Experiments by Hung and Plott (2001), Drehmann et al. (2007) and Owens (2011) have studied herding with direct payoff externalities and found that subjects are more responsive to these than to informational externalities.

[3]Weizsacker's (2010) meta-study of 13 herding experiments reveals that subjects make the empirically optimally choice 44% of the time when it contradicts private information but 90% of the time when it is consistent with private information. Celen and Kariv (2005) find that subjects are even more likely to overweight private information when they observe only the choice of their immediate predecessor, as in my experiment, than when they observe the entire sequence of preceding choices. In contrast, Dominitz and Hung (2009) elicit beliefs in a replication of prior experiments and find that patterns in discrete choice data are better explained by heterogeneous belief updating than systematic overweighting of private information.

the choices they observe others make.

The Restaurant Game is a useful setting for testing this explanation. It involves a sequence of four players choosing between alternatives with a capacity of two. Each player receives a private signal, which along with the observed choice of the preceding player can help her form expectations about the relative quality of the alternatives. The third and fourth players incur a "waiting cost" if they choose the same alternative as at least two preceding players. In the experiment, the choices of the first two players are made by computers with fixed decision rules, allowing me to test the extent to which the common deviation from Nash equilibrium is consistent with rational expectations given that predecessors sometimes make errors.[4] Results of the experiment confirm that the capacity constraint and waiting cost make the third player less likely to follow preceding players, as predicted by the Nash equilibrium. Because the problem of avoiding the waiting cost is more complex for the fourth player, the behavior of subjects in this role is more heterogeneous. I find that reducing strategic uncertainty by using computer players early in sequences does increase social learning by later players, but deviations from Nash equilibrium persist.

The complexity of the fourth player's problem and the heterogeneity in observed strategies provide a context for exploring the role of Level-$k$ thinking and cognitive ability in herding behavior. When the waiting cost is high, he is predicted to choose contrary to the third player unconditional on his private signal if he is Level-1, whereas he is predicted to follow the third player unconditional on his private signal for Level-2 and higher (including the Nash equilibrium). I find that a substantial proportion of strategies are consistent with each prediction. I also find a within-subject correlation between proximity to the Level-1 prediction in this high-cost setting and proximity to Level-1 in the standard no-cost setting. These results suggest that the commonly observed bias in herding behavior can be explained by a substantial proportion of subjects who engage in Level-1 thinking.

---

[4]See error-rate response models such as the Quantal Response Equilibrium of McKelvey and Palfrey (1995). Anderson and Holt (1997), Anderson (2001), Goeree et al. (2007) and Ziegelmeyer et al. (2010) find evidence that this concept can explain deviations from equilibrium in herding environments. Kubler and Weizsacker (2004) and Brunner and Goeree (2011) find that response to error-rates alone cannot explain biases in their herding experiments, but this concept does fit the data when modified to incorporate limited depth-of-reasoning. Ivanov et al. (2009) find that boundedly-rational rules of thumb explain behavior better than Quantal Response. A similar alternative explanation is that individuals are overconfident in their private information causing them to discount information given to them by others, but Celen et al. (2010) find disconfirming evidence that direct advice leads to strategies closer to the equilibrium than strategies with social learning alone.

Moreover, I find evidence that the fourth player's strategies are significantly closer to the Nash equilibrium and significantly farther from the Level-1 strategy when the subject's ACT scores are in the top 5% of all test-takers, an indicator of high cognitive ability.

The paper proceeds as follows. Section 2 describes the Restaurant Game and its Nash equilibrium, while Section 3 explains the experimental design and the Level-$k$ predictions. Section 4 states the main research questions, Section 5 reports the experimental results, and Section 6 concludes.

# 2   The Restaurant Game

The Restaurant Game[5] is a model of herding with continuous signals[6] and imperfect information about predecessors' choices[7] with the addition of capacity constraints. Four players, indexed by $n \in \{1, 2, 3, 4\}$, arrive on a boulevard in sequence and choose between two restaurants, Ray's ($R$) and Louie's ($L$), in order of arrival. The restaurant choice of player $n$ is denoted by $x_n \in \{R, L\}$. Before choosing, each player receives a noisy private signal about the relative quality of the food at the restaurants, $\theta_n$, drawn independently and uniformly from the interval $[0, 1]$, and observes the choice of only the immediately preceding player, $x_{n-1}$. The true quality of $R$'s food is equal to $\frac{\sum_{i=1}^{4} \theta_i}{4}$, while the true quality of $L$'s food is equal to $1 - \frac{\sum_{i=1}^{4} \theta_i}{4}$. Each restaurant can serve only two players at a time, so if Player 3 or Player 4 chooses the same restaurant as at least two of the preceding players then that player incurs the cost of waiting for a table. Player $n$'s payoff from choosing a restaurant is equal to the true quality of the chosen restaurant's food minus that player's waiting cost, $C_n(x_1, ..., x_n)$, which is equal to $c \in [0, 1]$ if at least two of $n$'s predecessors chose the same restaurant and 0 otherwise.

Suppose $x_{n-1} = R$. Player $n$ chooses restaurant $R$ if and only if the following holds:

$$E[U(\tfrac{\sum_{i=1}^{4} \theta_i}{4} - C_n(x_1, ..., x_{n-1}, R))|\theta_n, x_{n-1} = R]$$
$$\geq E[U(1 - \tfrac{\sum_{i=1}^{4} \theta_i}{4} - C_n(x_1, ..., x_{n-1}, L))|\theta_n, x_{n-1} = R].$$

---

[5]The restaurant-choice framing for herding games originates with Banerjee (1992) and has been used more recently by Eyster and Rabin (2010). This game is also similar to the El Farol bar problem of Arthur (1994).
[6]See Smith and Sorensen (2000), Celen and Kariv (2004a, 2004b, 2005) and Owens (2011).
[7]See Celen and Kariv (2004b, 2005).

By monotonicity of $U$ in $\theta_n$, it follows that player $n$ uses a decision rule given by:

$$x_n(x_{n-1} = R) = \begin{cases} R & \text{if } \theta_n \geq \hat{\theta}_n(c) \\ L & \text{if } \theta_n < \hat{\theta}_n(c) \end{cases}.$$

The problem is symmetric for $x_{n-1} = L$, so in this case player $n$ follows a decision rule given by:

$$x_n(x_{n-1} = L) = \begin{cases} R & \text{if } \theta_n \geq 1 - \hat{\theta}_n(c) \\ L & \text{if } \theta_n < 1 - \hat{\theta}_n(c) \end{cases}.$$

Therefore, the equilibrium is fully characterized by $\hat{\theta}_n(c)$ for each $n$. I refer to $\hat{\theta}_n(c)$ as player $n$'s equilibrium strategy at waiting cost $c$.

The risk-neutral Bayesian Nash equilibrium strategies, $\hat{\theta}_n(c)$, for the four players are as follows (see Appendix A for derivations):

$$\hat{\theta}_1(c) = \frac{1}{2}; \hat{\theta}_2(c) = \frac{1}{4}; \hat{\theta}_3(c) = \begin{cases} \frac{3+24c}{16} & \text{if } c \leq \frac{13}{24} \\ 1 & \text{if } c > \frac{13}{24} \end{cases}; \hat{\theta}_4(c) = \begin{cases} \frac{1}{256}(39 + 368c - 576c^2) & \text{if } c \leq \frac{13}{24} \\ \frac{13-16c}{16} & \text{if } c \in (\frac{13}{24}, \frac{13}{16}] \\ 0 & \text{if } c > \frac{13}{16} \end{cases}.$$

Consider a simple example demonstrating the Nash strategies of P1 and P2. Suppose that P1 receives a private signal of .62 and P2 receives a private signal of .41. Because there are no players preceding P1 and her private signal is greater than .5, she expects the payoff of choosing R (the average of the four players' private signals) to be greater than the payoff of L (1 minus the average of the four players' private signals). P1 chooses R, and P2 observes P1's choice. By observing that P1 chooses R, P2 infers that P1's private signal is between .5 and 1. Because P2's expectation of P1's signal is .75, he expects the payoff of choosing R (the average of the four players' private signals) to be greater than the payoff of L (1 minus the average of the four players' private signals) unless he receives a strong disagreeing private signal less than .25. Because P2's private signal is .41, he chooses R as well.

Figure 2.1: Nash Strategies for Players 3 and 4

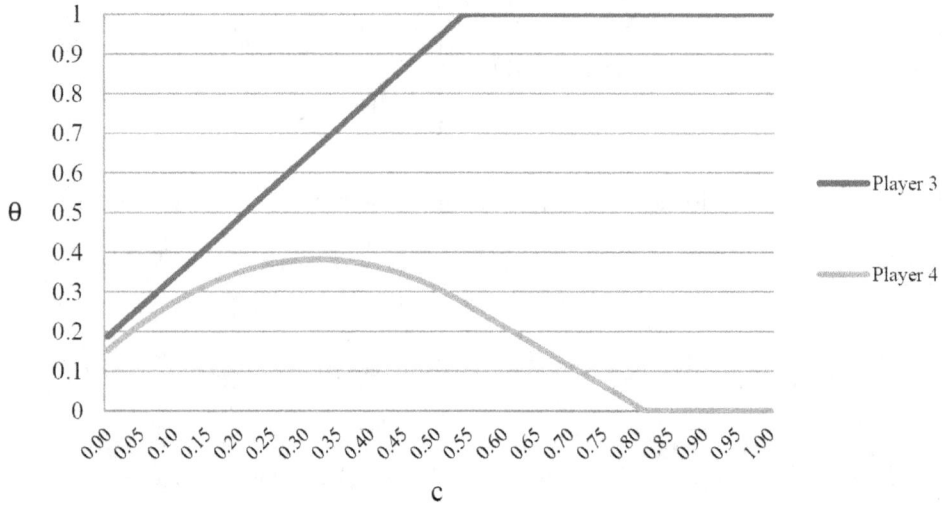

The Nash strategies for Players 3 and 4, $\hat{\theta}_3(c)$ and $\hat{\theta}_4(c)$, are shown in Figure 2.1. For low waiting costs, Player 3 (P3) follows Player 2 (P2) if her private signal agrees with P2's choice[8] or if it disagrees but not too strongly. Player 4's (P4's) strategy at low costs is similar, except that the informational externality of P3's choice is slightly larger than that of P2's, so P4 follows P3 for a slightly larger range of private signals. As the waiting cost increases, the incentive to avoid the cost attenuates herding, so the range of private signals for which P3 follows P2 and the range for which P4 follows P3 shrink. The range of signals for which P3 follows P2 continues to shrink until the waiting cost is sufficiently high that the incentive to avoid it dominates the incentive to choose the highest-quality restaurant. In this region, P3 chooses contrary to P2 unconditional on her private signal.

Unlike P3's, P4's Nash strategy is non-monotonic in the waiting cost. Because increasing the cost raises the likelihood that P3 chooses contrary to P2, and because P2 follows Player 1 (P1) with probability 3/4, increasing the cost raises the likelihood that P4 can avoid it by *following* P3. At the same time, increasing the cost makes avoiding it more important, so the range of signals for which P4 follows P3 begins to expand with the cost when it is sufficiently high. Beyond this point, the range of signals for which P4 follows P3 continues to expand until it reaches the level where

---

[8]Player $n$'s signal "agrees" with Player $n-1$'s choice when $\theta_n \geq 0.5$ if $x_{n-1} = R$ and when $\theta_n \leq 0.5$ if $x_{n-1} = L$.

the incentive to avoid the cost dominates the incentive to choose the highest-quality restaurant. In this region, P4 follows P3 unconditional on his private signal.

# 3   Experimental Design and Level-$k$ Strategies

In this section, I describe the four treatments of the experiment: BASE, ORDER, 1-2-L1 and 1-2-H. Table 3.1 summarizes the key features of each treatment. I also consider how strategies may differ from the Nash equilibrium in each treatment if subjects do not learn from the observed choices of others in a way consistent with full, commonly known rationality. The Level-$k$ model[9] provides a natural representation of such bounded rationality. In the Level-$k$ model, players choose a best-response given non-equilibrium beliefs about the rationality of others. A Level-0 player chooses an action randomly, a Level-1 player best-responds to the belief that others are Level-0, a Level-2 player best-responds to the belief that others are Level-1, and a Level-$k$ player best-responds to the belief that others are Level-$k-1$.[10] Level-$k$ strategies are the same in BASE and ORDER but different in the other treatments, so I describe the design and Level-$k$ strategies of these treatments first and return to 1-2-L1 and 1-2-H later.

## 3.1   Treatments BASE and ORDER

The purpose of BASE is to explore the behavior of subjects in the roles of P3 and P4 while P1 and P2 are computer players, with cost levels played in random sequence to control for order effects. ORDER is identical to BASE except that the cost levels are played in increasing rather than random sequence, allowing a comparison with previous literature by capturing behavior in the standard no-cost setting before prompting responses to the capacity constraint and waiting cost.

Sessions of BASE and ORDER consist of 18 rounds. In each round, subjects are matched

---

[9]See Stahl and Wilson (1994), Nagel (1995), Costa-Gomes et al. (2001), Camerer et al. (2004), Costa-Gomes and Crawford (2006) and Crawford and Iriberri (2007).

[10]The Level-1 concept closely resembles the Cursed Equilibrium of Eyster and Rabin (2005), and in fact the Level-1 and Cursed Equilibrium strategies are identical in this model. Similarly, the Level-2 prediction is identical to the Best Response Trailing Naive Inference Equilibrium of Eyster and Rabin (2010). As discussed in Eyster and Rabin (2009), Cursed Equilibrium and Level-1 predictions coincide in most cases (as do the Best Response Trailing Naive Inference Equilibrium and Level-2 predictions), but Level-1 players believe that other players' choices are uniformly distributed while Cursed players' beliefs can take any arbitrary distribution.

Table 3.1: Treatments

| Treatment | Order of Cost Levels | Player 1 | Player 2 |
|-----------|---------------------|----------|----------|
| BASE | Random | Nash Computer | Nash Computer |
| ORDER | No, Low, High | Nash Computer | Nash Computer |
| 1-2-L1 | Random | Level-1 Computer | Level-1 Computer |
| 1-2-H | Random | Human Subject | Human Subject |

randomly and anonymously in pairs: one subject with the role of P3 and the other with the role of P4. P3 and P4 make a choice in each round after choices are made by two computer players, P1 and P2. P3 and P4 roles are assigned randomly to subjects at the beginning of the experiment, and subjects keep the same role throughout.

Each round has exactly the same rules as the Restaurant Game presented in Section 2, except that the parameters are multiplied by 100 and the restaurant framing is replaced by neutral language.[11] Each player chooses one of two options, R and L, in sequence. The strategies followed by computer players P1 and P2 are shown to subjects using a diagram, which is reproduced in the left panel of Figure 3.1. In BASE and ORDER, P1 and P2 choose according to their Nash strategies. Before choosing, P3 and P4 subjects see only the cost for that round and the choice of the immediately preceding player on their computer screens.

The experiment uses a belief elicitiation procedure for entering choices,[12] in which subjects are asked to enter a number between 0 and 100 before learning their private signal. If the private signal turns out to be greater than this number, the subject's choice is $R$, and if the private signal turns out to be less than this number, the subject's choice is $L$. After a number is entered, the private signal is drawn and shown on the subject's computer screen along with the resulting choice, the payoff associated with this choice, the cost incurred (if any) and net earnings for the round.

In each round, the cost is set at one of three values: 0, 35 or 85. In my analysis, I refer to them as No-Cost, Low-Cost or High-Cost rounds, respectively. Six of the 18 rounds in each session are played at each cost level. In BASE, the sequence in which these rounds are played is determined randomly. In ORDER, the No-Cost rounds are played first, followed by the Low-Cost rounds and

---

[11]See Appendix B for the instructions and screenshots seen by subjects. The experimental software is programmed in zTree (Fischbacher, 2007).

[12]This method has been used in previous continuous-signal herding experiments by Celen and Kariv (2004a, 2005), Celen et al. (2010) and Owens (2011).

8

Figure 3.1: Computer Player Strategies

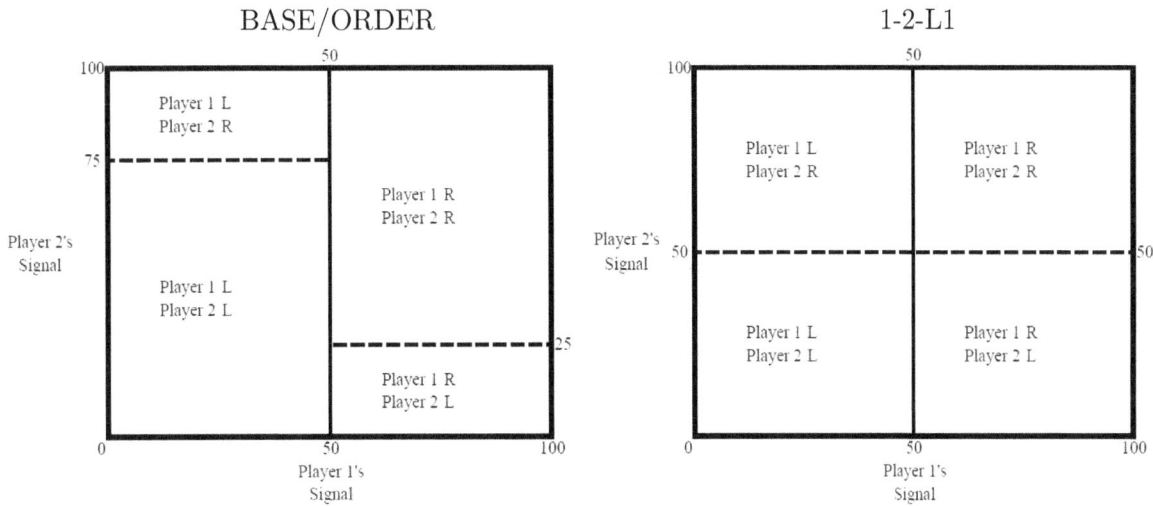

finally the High-Cost rounds.[13] Payoffs are denominated in Experimental Currency Units (ECUs). Subjects receive a starting balance of 50 ECUs plus their earnings in one randomly determined round out of the six played at each cost level (three rounds total). They are paid cash at an exchange rate of $0.10 per ECU, in addition to a fixed participation fee of $5.

Because P1 and P2 are computers whose choice rules are fixed and known to all human players in the experiment, it seems implausible that P3 and P4 would have inconsistent beliefs about the behavior of these players. However, P4's beliefs about the rationality of human subjects in the role of P3 may lead to behavior consistent with Level-$k$ predictions. That is, a Level-$k$ P4 may best-respond to the belief that P1 and P2 follow their programmed strategies and P3 follows a Level-$k-1$ strategy. The Level-$k$ strategies of P4 in BASE and ORDER are shown in Figure 3.2.

P4's Level-$k$ strategies coincide with the Nash for Level-4 and higher, and his Level-2 and Level-3 strategies are very close to his Nash strategy in these treatments. On Level-2 and higher, P4 believes that P3's choice in No-Cost rounds reveals some information about her private signal and, on Level-3 and higher, about the private signals of P1 and P2 also. However, a Level-1 P4 believes that P3 chooses randomly, and he best-responds to that belief by choosing based entirely on his

---

[13]Two trial rounds which do not count for payment precede these 18 rounds so that subjects can become familiar with the software interface. In ORDER, the cost level is 0 in both trial rounds. In the other three treatments, the cost level in trial rounds is drawn randomly and independently from {0, 35, 85}.

Figure 3.2: Player 4 Level-$k$ Strategies in BASE/ORDER

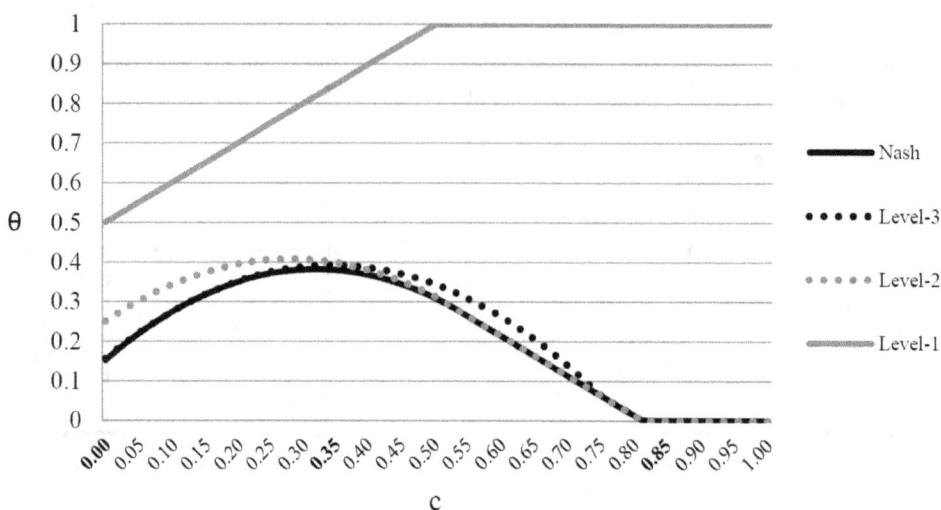

own private information. Hence, the overweighting of private information observed in the herding literature is consistent with Level-1 thinking, as distinguished from Level-2 and higher.

The advantage of this design lies in the divergence between Level-1 and higher levels, which predict strategies at opposite endpoints of the strategy interval in High-Cost rounds. On all levels higher than Level-1, P4 recognizes that P3 always chooses contrary to P2 in High-Cost rounds and that P1 chooses the same as P2 with probability 3/4. Because the incentive to avoid the waiting cost dominates in these rounds, it is optimal for P4 to follow P3 unconditional on his private signal given these beliefs. However, the Level-1 P4 believes that P3's choice reveals nothing about the choice of P2 or P1 and he is most likely to avoid the waiting cost by choosing contrary to P3. Hence, the Level-1 P4 chooses contrary to P3 unconditional on his private signal in High-Cost rounds.

## 3.2   Treatment 1-2-L1

Treatment 1-2-L1 is identical to BASE except that the choices of computer players P1 and P2 are independent rather than correlated, which changes P4 predictions for Level-2 and higher but not Level-1. Results from 1-2-L1 and BASE can then be compared to determine whether P4 behavior responds to differences in these predictions between the two treatments.

In 1-2-L1, P1 and P2 both choose based entirely on their own private signals by using a strategy

Figure 3.3: Player 4 Level-$k$ Strategies in 1-2-L1

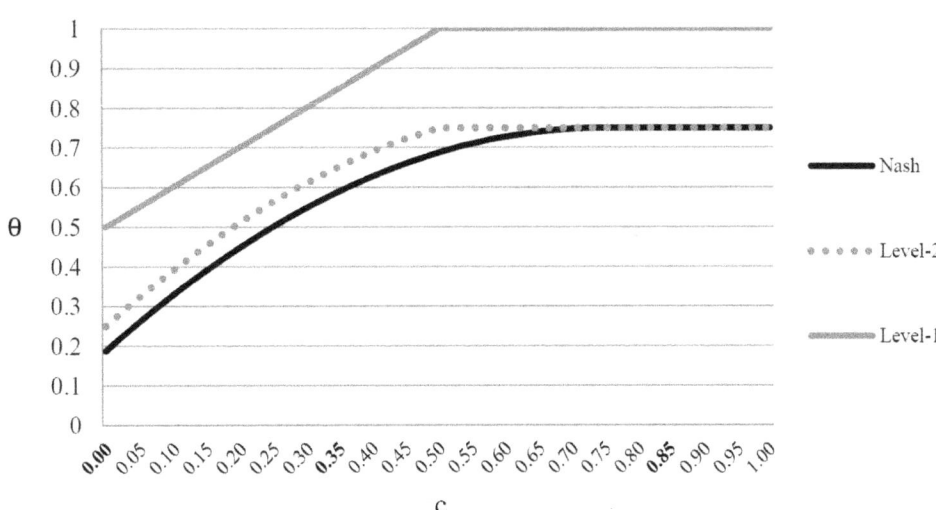

of 50. Their strategies are represented to subjects in this treatment as shown in the right panel of Figure 3.1. Because the choices of P1 and P2 are independent in this treatment but not in the others, fewer iterations of best-response are involved before players reach the Nash equilibrium. The strategies of computer players P1 and P2 thus correspond to what would be the Level-1 strategy for human players in this treatment, which means that P3's Nash strategy would concide with Level-2 ($\hat{\theta}_3^{L2}(c) = \frac{1+4c}{4}$ if $c \leq \frac{3}{4}$ and $\hat{\theta}_3^{L2}(c) = 1$ if $c > \frac{3}{4}$) and P4's Nash strategy with Level-3.

The Level-$k$ strategies of P4 in 1-2-L1 are shown in Figure 3.3. His Level-1 strategy is the same as in the other treatments. For Level-2 and higher, P4 recognizes that P3 always chooses contrary to P2 in High-Cost rounds, but P1 chooses the same as P2 with probability 1/2 rather than 3/4 in this treatment, so P2's choice now reveals nothing about P1's. Therefore, P4 cannot expect to avoid the waiting cost by following P3 in High-Cost rounds; he is equally likely to incur the cost by following as he is by choosing contrary to P3. Hence, P4's choice is based on his own private signal and what he infers about P2's private signal from P3's choice. He follows P2 by choosing contrary to P3 in High-Cost rounds unless his own private signal strongly disagrees with P2's inferred choice.

Figure 3.4: Player 3 Level-$k$ Strategies in 1-2-H

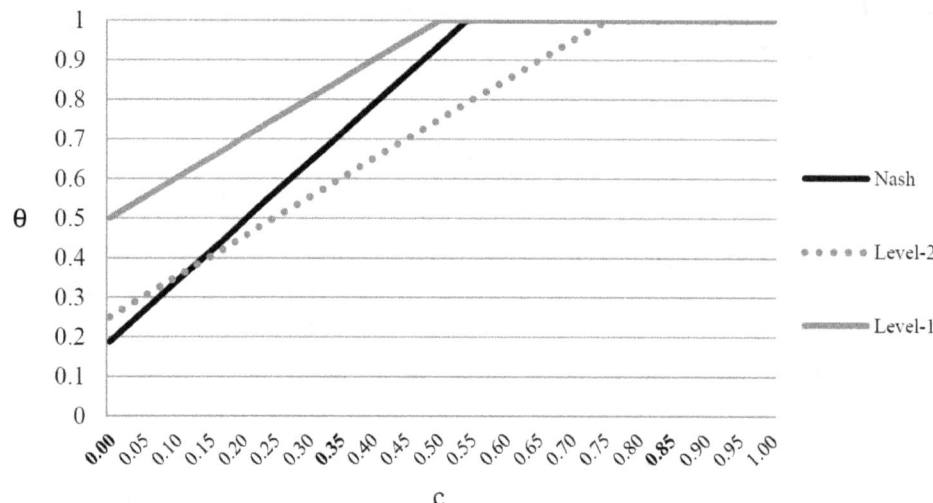

## 3.3   Treatment 1-2-H

Treatment 1-2-H differs from the other three treatments in that P1 and P2 are human subjects instead of computer players. Results of the other treatments can be compared to those of 1-2-H to determine the extent to which deviations from Nash equilibrium can be attributed to uncertainty about the strategies of P1 and P2.

In this treatment, P1, P2, P3 and P4 roles are assigned randomly to subjects at the beginning of the experiment, and subjects keep the same role throughout. In each of the 12 rounds of this treatment, subjects are matched with one player in each other role and make choices in sequence accordingly. Four rounds are played at each cost level, and one of the four rounds at each cost level is chosen randomly for payment. Cost levels are played in a randomly determined order.

Because all four players in a sequence are humans in 1-2-H, both P3 and P4 may hold inconsistent beliefs about the behavior of P1 and P2 in this treatment. The Level-$k$ strategies of P3 and P4 in this treatment are shown in Figures 3.4 and 3.5, respectively. Their Level-1 strategies are the same because these strategies condition choices on only the private signal and action of the immediately preceding player. P3's Level-2 strategy is the same as her Nash (and Level-2) strategy in 1-2-L1 and P4's Level-2 strategy is the same as his Level-2 strategy in 1-2-L1 because computer players P1 and P2 follow what would be their Level-1 strategies in 1-2-L1. P4's Level-3 and Nash

Figure 3.5: Player 4 Level-$k$ Strategies in 1-2-H

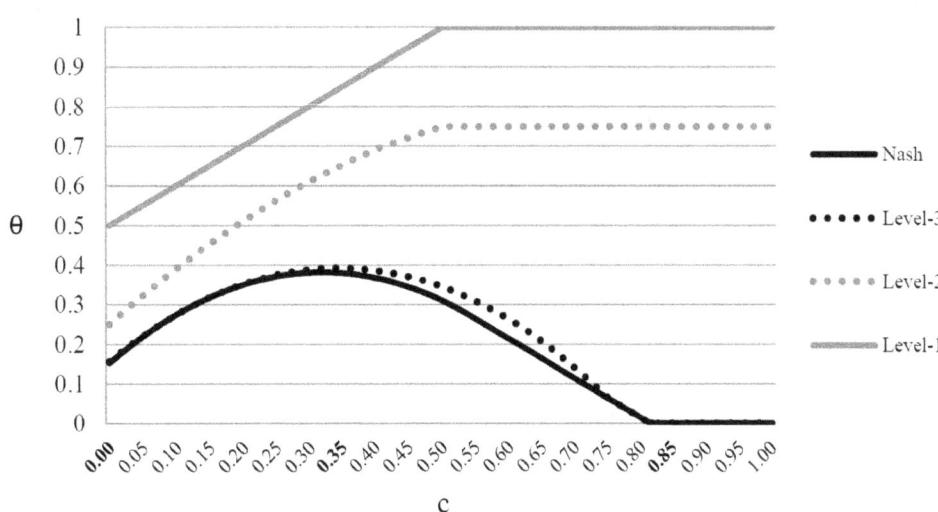

strategies are the same as in BASE and ORDER because they best-respond to beliefs that P1's and P2's strategies are the same as those played by computer players P1 and P2 in those treatments, with P3 following her Level-2 or Nash strategy, respectively.

# 4    Research Questions

*Question 1: How does the capacity constraint affect the strategies of Players 3 and 4?*

The Nash equilibrium predicts that capacity constraints attenuate herding behavior, as the incentive to avoid the waiting cost works against the incentive to choose the highest-quality alternative. When the waiting cost is low, the capacity constraint is predicted to shift P3 strategies such that following P2 is less likely but remains conditional on her private signal. When it is high, P3 is predicted to choose contrary to P2 unconditional on her private signal. For P4, the waiting cost is predicted to have a non-monotonic effect on strategies in BASE, ORDER and 1-2-H. When the waiting cost is high, P4 is predicted to follow P3 unconditional on his private signal in BASE, ORDER and 1-2-H, while he is predicted to choose contrary to P3 for all disagreeing and weak agreeing signals in 1-2-L1.

*Question 2: Compared to when preceding choices are made by humans, do strategies exhibit more social learning when predecessors are computers with fixed, commonly known strategies?*

Herding experiments typically study how choices are influenced by learning from preceding choices made by human subjects. In contrast with this convention, P3 in the BASE, ORDER and 1-2-L1 treatments of this experiment makes a choice given information about the choices of computer players whose strategies are fixed and commonly known. This feature of the design allows me to test the hypothesis that subjects in herding experiments overweight private information due to the possibility that preceding human players make errors. To address this issue, I compare P3 and P4 strategies in BASE to those in 1-2-H, which is identical to BASE except that P1 and P2 are human subjects. This comparison allows an assessment of the degree to which overweighting of private information relative to the Nash is caused by rational expectations of human behavior. I also compare my results to those of Celen and Kariv's (2005) experiment,[14] in which the environment for P3 and P4 is equivalent to No-Cost rounds of 1-2-H, though the instructions and parameter scale differ.

*Question 3: Does Level-k thinking explain departures from Nash equilibrium?*

In contrast to standard herding models, the game explored in BASE and ORDER affords the advantage of a particularly clear distinction between Level-1 strategies and strategies of Level-2 and higher when the waiting cost is high. Hence, these treatments are well-suited to test the predictions of the Level-$k$ model and also allow a test of their within-subject robustness across different settings. Comparison of results from 1-2-L1, where the choices of P1 and P2 are independent, and BASE, where they are correlated, should also shed light on how the behavior of P4 responds to Level-$k$ predictions. P4's Level-1 strategy in both BASE and 1-2-L1 is to choose contrary to P3 unconditional on his private signal. His strategy on Level-2 and higher in BASE is to follow P3 unconditional on his private signal, but in 1-2-L1 it is to choose contrary to P3 for all but strong agreeing signals. Comparison of the data with these stark differences in predictions can shed light

---

[14]I thank the authors of this paper for sharing their data.

on whether Level-$k$ thinking is responsible for the bias observed in herding games.

*Question 4: Is there a relationship between subjects' cognitive ability and the proximity of their strategies to theoretical predictions?*

I consider both the fully-rational Nash equilibrium and boundedly-rational Level-$k$ strategies as candidate models of behavior in this experiment. Given that some heterogeneity in behavior is found in the data, it may be that the degree to which subjects behave as predicted by the alternative theories is determined by their cognitive ability. I investigate the relationship between the proximity of subjects' strategies to the Nash, Level-1 and Level-2 predictions and their cognitive ability, as indicated by American College Test (ACT) and Scholastic Aptitude Test (SAT) scores. ACT and SAT scores have been shown by Frey and Detterman (2004) and Koenig et al. (2008), respectively, to be strongly correlated with measures of general intelligence. Comparing these scores with the experimental data may provide an explanation for observed differences in levels of thinking.

# 5   Experimental Results

Sessions were conducted at the Ohio State University Experimental Economics Lab in the fall of 2011 and spring of 2012. A total of 298 subjects participated in the experiment with 86 participating in BASE over 4 sessions, 78 participating in ORDER over 3 sessions, 78 participating in 1-2-L1 over 3 sessions and 56 participating in 1-2-H over 2 sessions. All subjects participated in only one of the treatments, so all treatment differences are between-subject, while differences between No-Cost, Low-Cost and High-Cost rounds in each treatment are within-subject. Subjects were recruited with email invitations sent out randomly to students in a large database of Ohio State undergraduates of all majors. Sessions lasted between 60 and 90 minutes, with average earnings of $22.15.

The advantage of the strategy-elicitation method used in the experiment is that it allows me to determine proximity to the different theoretical predictions and to infer the degree to which strategies rely on private information vs. social learning. Due to the symmetry of the model and the observed behavior, I simplify the analysis henceforth by normalizing the data to one dimension

Table 5.1: Predicted vs. Actual Effects of Treatment and Cost Level

| BASE/ORDER Prediction | | No-Cost | Low-Cost | High-Cost | 1-2-L1 Prediction | | No-Cost | Low-Cost | High-Cost |
|---|---|---|---|---|---|---|---|---|---|
| Nash | P3 | 19 | 71 | 100 | Nash | P3 | 25 | 60 | 100 |
| | P4 | 15 | 38 | 0 | | P4 | 19 | 59 | 75 |
| Level-2 | P4 | 25 | 40 | 0 | Level-2 | P4 | 25 | 65 | 75 |
| Level-1 | P4 | 50 | 85 | 100 | Level-1 | P4 | 50 | 85 | 100 |
| Mean Strategy | | No-Cost | Low-Cost | High-Cost | Mean Strategy | | No-Cost | Low-Cost | High-Cost |
| BASE | P3 | 44.5 <<< | 69.3 | 71.9 | 1-2-L1 | P3 | 43.2 <<< | 70.7 <<< | 80.2 |
| | P4 | 53.3 | 55.5 | 53.1 | | P4 | 52.2 << | 59.3 | 63.6 |
| ORDER | P3 | 45.3 <<< | 64.5 <<< | 77.6 | 1-2-H† | P3 | 53.4 <<< | 76.0 | 83.2 |
| | P4 | 42.1*** | 46.9 | 46.1 | | P4 | 51.6 | 65.3 | 67.5 |

Between-cost-level difference significant at: <<< .01 level, << .05 level, < .1 level.
Between-treatment difference (compared to BASE) significant at: *** .01 level, ** .05 level, * .1 level.
†1-2-H: Nash same as BASE/ORDER; Level-2 same as P3 Nash/P4 Level-2 in 1-2-L1; Level-1 same as P4 Level-1s.

of strategies which combines the strategies entered when the preceding player chose R with 100 minus the strategies entered when the preceding player chose L, and I analyze all of the strategies as if the preceding player chose R.[15] Table 5.1 reports the mean strategies entered by P3 and P4 in each treatment and cost level along with Nash and Level-$k$ predictions.[16] Figures 5.1 and 5.2 display the distributions of strategies in each treatment and cost level for P3 and P4, respectively, with the Nash prediction marked by a vertical line.

## 5.1 Response to Capacity Constraint

In this section, I study how the capacity constraint and waiting cost level affect the strategies of Players 3 and 4 by comparing differences in their mean strategies between cost levels to the differences predicted by the Nash equilibrium.[17]

---

[15]Figures C.1 and C.2 in Appendix C display the distributions of strategies entered by P3 and P4 subjects in each treatment split by cost level and the choice of the immediately preceding player (R or L). These figures show that the distribution of strategies when the preceding player chose R and the distribution when the preceding player chose L are reasonably symmetric, with no consistent bias towards R or L. Kolmogorov-Smirnov tests find no significant differences in the distribution of strategies when the preceding player chose R and the mirror image of the distribution when the preceding player chose L in any treatment/cost level combination, except for P3 in No-Cost rounds of ORDER and 1-2-L1 and for P4 in Low-Cost rounds of BASE, where the difference is accounted for by a few subjects who always enter a strategy of 100 in these rounds.

[16]Table C.1 in Appendix C reports the mean strategies in subjects' first and last of the six rounds played at each cost level in each treatment for both P3 and P4. Mean strategies entered by both P3 and P4 in BASE and 1-2-H show a consistent shift towards the Nash between the first and last round played at each cost level, but the data from ORDER and 1-2-L1 do not exhibit this tendency.

[17]I use Wilcoxon signed-ranks tests to determine whether the capacity constraint and waiting cost have the predicted within-subject effects on strategies. Observations for these tests are subject-level mean strategies at each cost level.

Figure 5.1: Distribution of Player 3 Strategies by Treatment and Cost Level

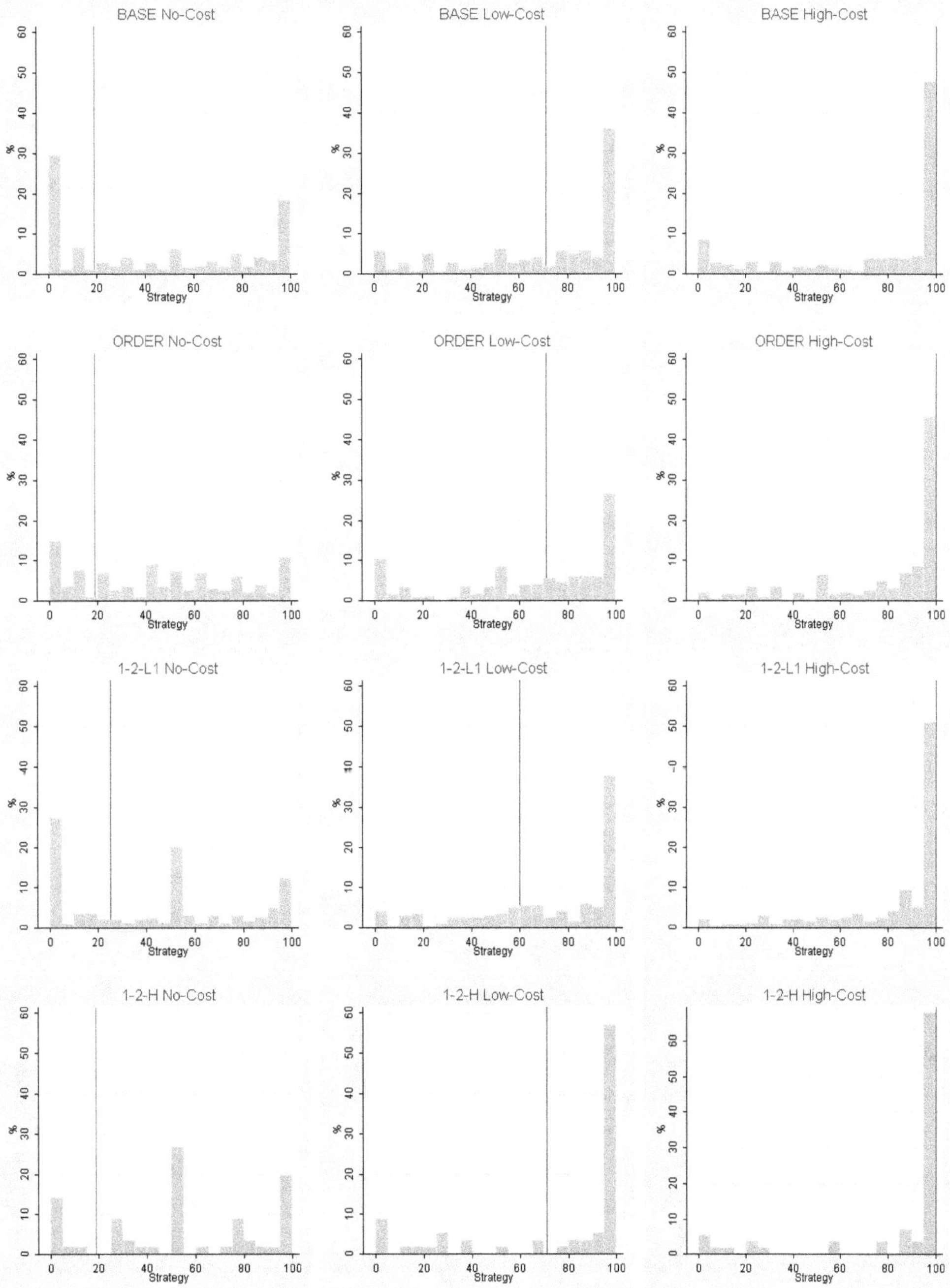

17

Figure 5.2: Distribution of Player 4 Strategies by Treatment and Cost Level

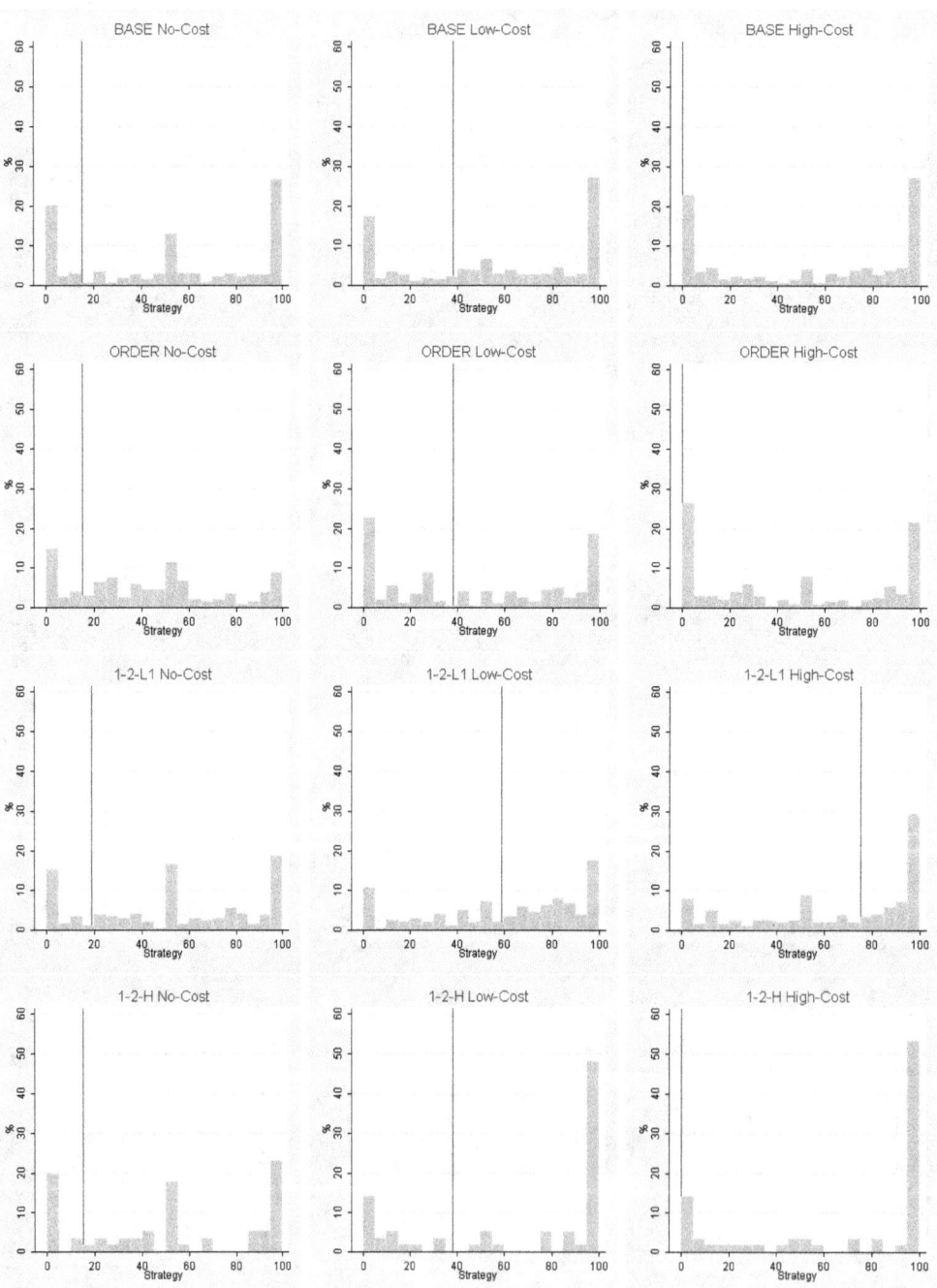

*Result 1.1: Player 3 behavior is generally consistent with the comparative static effects of the capacity constraint and waiting cost level predicted by the Nash equilibrium.*

I find that both imposing the capacity constraint with a low waiting cost and raising the waiting cost from low to high attenuate herding behavior, as predicted by the Nash equilibrium. P3 strategies are such that following P2 is less likely with a low waiting cost than with no waiting cost and less likely with a high waiting cost than a low waiting cost. Differences between P3's mean No-Cost and Low-Cost strategies are statistically significant in all treatments, but differences between her Low-Cost and High-Cost strategies are statistically significant in ORDER and 1-2-L1 only.[18]

*Result 1.2: When the Nash equilibrium corresponds to Level-3 rather than Level-4, Player 4 behavior is consistent with the predicted comparative static effect of the capacity constraint.*

Results for P4 are also consistent with Nash comparative static predictions in 1-2-L1, where the choices of P1 and P2 are independent. In this treatment, P4's Low-Cost strategies are significantly higher than his No-Cost strategies, making him less likely to follow P3 with a low waiting cost than with no waiting cost. Because the choices of P1 and P2 are independent in this treatment, fewer iterations of best-response are required to reach Nash than in the others. In 1-2-L1, P4's Nash strategy corresponds to Level-3, while in the other three treatments it corresponds to Level-4. Hence, P4 responds to the capacity constraint as predicted when the Nash strategy involves a lower level of thinking.

---

[18]Using Wilcoxon rank-sum tests taking subject-level means as the unit of observation, I find no significant differences between P3's mean strategies in BASE and the other treatments. The same is true for P4, except that P4's mean No-Cost strategy is significantly lower in ORDER than in BASE. Because the underlying game is identical in BASE and ORDER, I should observe no differences between these two treatments unless behavior is affected by the order in which cost levels are played. I find evidence that this difference is due to hysteresis of strategies across cost levels when they are played in random sequence. Though the proportion of No-Cost strategies equal to 0 or 100 in ORDER (16.6%) is similar to the rate of such strategies in Celen and Kariv (2005) (17.5%), the proportions of such strategies in BASE (30.3%) and 1-2-L1 (28.0%) are much higher. Hence, strategies in rounds with an interior equilibrium are distributed more in the interior of the interval when these rounds are played before rounds with a corner equilibrium (ORDER) than when rounds are played in random sequence (BASE/1-2-L1). Because P4's mean No-Cost strategy is a more meaningful representation of P4 behavior in ORDER than in the other treatments, it is not surprising that the mean is significantly closer to the Nash strategy in this treatment than in the others.

## 5.2 Social Learning with Computers vs. Human Players

In this section, I ask whether strategies exhibit more social learning when P1 and P2 are computers with fixed, commonly known strategies than when they are human subjects. In the standard No-Cost setting of all four treatments, mean strategies of P3 and P4 overweight private information compared to the Nash prediction.[19] None of the mean No-Cost strategies are significantly less than 50 at the .1 level., where 50 is the strategy which makes a choice based entirely on the private signal.[20] However, the distributions of strategies in Figures 5.1 and 5.2 reveal that behavior varies widely in some treatments and cost levels, particularly for P4, whose distributions are largely bimodal. This finding raises an important methodological issue in analyzing herding experiments that use strategy elicitation: the mean strategies may not tell the whole story, so the distributions of strategies must be studied.[21] To study between-treatment differences in these distributions, I compare the proportions of observed strategies within an interval of 5 about a given benchmark. This approach allows for some error about the benchmark while maintaining a 95% chance that strategies in the chosen interval choose the same action as the benchmark strategy.[22]

*Result 2: When the first two players are humans, more strategies condition only on private information and less strategies condition only on social learning than when they are computers.*

In 1-2-H, strategies of human subjects in both P1 and P2 roles vary widely, with standard deviations of 25.9 and 31.5, respectively. The mean strategy for P1 is 50.3, almost exactly matching

---

[19]In Appendix D, I explore the impact of risk aversion on the Bayesian Nash equilibrium. Risk-aversion generally has a negligible impact on equilibrium strategies, so this does not appear to explain the observed deviations from Nash predictions.

[20]This result is consistent with those of other studies with human preceding players such as Celen and Kariv (2005), who report means equivalent to 44.6 for P3 and 43.8 for P4 in terms of my parameters.

[21]A substantial proportion of subjects in both roles use No-Cost strategies which are not even minimally consistent with the Nash, choosing contrary to their immediate predecessor given an agreeing private signal. In Appendix E, I study the strategies of those subjects whose mean No-Cost strategy satisfies basic rationality in the sense that it does not choose contrary to the immediate predecessor given an agreeing signal, i.e., the mean No-Cost strategy is less than or equal to 50. Among these subjects, P4 strategies are more consistent with equilibrium predictions but there is little difference for P3. I also find that for P4, measures of cognitive ability increase the likelihood of satisfying the basic rationality condition.

[22]For between-treatment differences in proportions of strategies falling within a given interval, I assess statistical significance as follows. An indicator variable is constructed taking the value 1 if a strategy falls in the specified interval and 0 otherwise. Observations are subject-level means of this indicator variable at each cost level. Wilcoxon rank-sum tests on these subject-level means determine significance.

the Nash prediction of 50, but the mean strategy for P2 is 39.6, significantly greater than the Nash prediction of 25 ($p = .0079$).[23] Because P1 and P2 are likely to deviate from the Nash strategy in this treatment, relying more on private information than the Nash equilibrium is consistent with rational expectations for P3 and P4. However, overweighting private information for this reason is not consistent with rational expectations in treatments where P1 and P2 are computer players.

Accordingly, the proportion of P3's No-Cost strategies that condition only on the private signal is higher when P1 and P2 are humans than when they are computers. The proportion of P3 strategies in the interval [47.5,52.5] is 23.2% in 1-2-H and 6.2% in BASE, though this difference is not statistically significant ($p = .2932$). I also find that the proportion of P3's No-Cost strategies that condition only on the preceding player's choice (overweighting social learning) is lower when P1 and P2 are humans than when they are computers. The proportion of P3's No-Cost strategies falling in the interval [0,5] is 14.3% in 1-2-H and 29.8% in BASE, a statistically significant difference ($p = 0.0782$). These findings indicate that reducing strategic uncertainty by using predictable computer players increases social learning, but inconsistency with Nash equilibrium persists.[24]

When preceding players are humans rather than computers, the tendency observed in No-Cost rounds to make choices based on factors other than social learning is also present in Low- and High-Cost rounds. In these rounds, this tendency is expressed in strategies which respond to the waiting cost by choosing contrary to the preceding player unconditionally. For both P3 and P4, the proportions of Low-Cost strategies in [95,100] are higher in 1-2-H than in BASE (57.1% vs. 36.0% for P3 ($p = 0.1466$) and 48.2% vs. 27.1% for P4 ($p = 0.0336$)). Similarly, the proportions of High-Cost strategies in [95,100] are higher in 1-2-H than in BASE for both players (67.9% vs. 47.7% for P3 ($p = 0.1163$) and 53.6% vs. 27.1% for P4 ($p = 0.0313$)).

## 5.3 Level-$k$ Behavior

In this section, I explore the extent to which the observed behavior is conisistent with Level-$k$ thinking as an alternative model of behavior to Nash equilibrium. P4 behavior that is consistent

---

[23]The distributions of these strategies are shown in Figure C.3 in Appendix C.

[24]March et al. (2012) also find that using computer players in a herding experiment increases social learning, but that even in this condition a substantial proportion of subjects overweight private information while others exhibit cascade behavior.

Table 5.2: Expected Payoffs of Player 4 Strategies Given Actual Player 3 Behavior

| Treatment | Cost | Empirically Optimal Strategy | Expected Payoff | | | |
|---|---|---|---|---|---|---|
| | | | Optimal | Nash | Level-1 | Level-2 |
| BASE | No | 47 | 55.7 | 52.6 | 55.3 | 52.8 |
| | Low | 36 | 39.0 | 37.0 | 37.2 | 37.4 |
| | High | 16 | 14.4 | 7.4 | 7.6 | 7.9 |
| ORDER | No | 36 | 58.7 | 56.4 | 57.3 | 56.3 |
| | Low | 79 | 46.4 | 45.6 | 40.7 | 45.3 |
| | High | 5 | 21.1 | 13.6 | 1.4 | 17.6 |
| 1-2-L1 | No | 41 | 56.8 | 54.2 | 54.4 | 55.3 |
| | Low | 73 | 42.4 | 41.0 | 40.2 | 40.7 |
| | High | 67 | 23.5 | 20.3 | 14.7 | 20.3 |

with Level-$k$ predictions is relatively easy to identify in High-Cost rounds of BASE and ORDER, where there is a maximum difference between the Level-1 strategy and the strategy of Level-2 and higher. I observe substantial proportions of strategies consistent with both. In High-Cost rounds of BASE and ORDER, respectively, 27.1% and 21.8% of P4 strategies fall in the interval [95,100], consistent with Level-1. Similar proportions (24.8% in BASE; 28.6% in ORDER) fall in the interval [0,5], consistent with Level-2 and higher.[25]

Before attributing these results to bounded rationality rather than rational expectations, it is necessary to determine what strategies would have been optimal for P4 given the actual behavior of preceding players. I determine the empirically optimal strategies for P4 at each cost level of BASE, ORDER and 1-2-L1 given the actual strategies of P1, P2 and P3 and the actual signal draws of all four players used in the experiment. Table 5.2 reports P4's optimal strategy at each cost level of these treatments along with his expected payoff per round from playing the empirically optimal, Nash, Level-1 and Level-2 strategies given the histories of play in the data.

*Result 3.1: The substantial proportion of strategies consistent with Level-1 when the waiting cost is high (27.1% in BASE, 21.8% in ORDER and 29.5% in 1-2-L1) are not rationalized by the actual behavior of preceding players.*

---

[25]Penczynski (2012) surveys the experimental herding literature through the lens of the level-$k$ model and finds that approximately 43% of the data from 13 different studies is consistent with Level-1, while much of the remaining data is consistent with Level-2.

22

Table 5.3: Player 4 Subjects in BASE/ORDER by Minimum Mean Absolute Deviation

| High-Cost | No-Cost Min. MAD | | |
|---|---|---|---|
| Min. MAD | Nash | Level-1 | Total |
| Nash | 19 (44.2%) | 24 (55.8%) | 43 |
| Level-1 | 9 (23.1%) | 30 (76.9%) | 39 |
| Total | 28 (34.1%) | 54 (65.9%) | 82 |

Percentage of row total in parentheses.

Given the realized signals and choices of preceding players in the experiment, there is little difference in expected payoff to P4 from playing each of the three predicted strategies. These expected payoffs are close to the expected payoff of the empirically optimal strategy in most cases. The exception is High-Cost rounds, where the expected payoff of the Level-1 strategy is substantially smaller than those of the empirically optimal strategies. In High-Cost rounds of BASE and ORDER, the empirically optimal strategies (16 in BASE; 5 in ORDER) are much closer to the Nash strategy (0) than the Level-1 strategy (100). Hence, in settings where the distribution of P4 strategies is bimodal, the Nash strategy performs better than Level-1 and is approximately optimal given the actual behavior of preceding players. This finding indicates that P4 strategies consistent with the Level-1 prediction are more plausibly attributed to bounded rationality than rational expectations.

Because of the heterogeneity of P4 strategies in High-Cost rounds of BASE and ORDER, it is useful to examine the subject-level data. If a subject's High-Cost strategies are clearly distinguished as consistent with Level-1 or with higher levels, the experimental design allows me to analyze how the same subject behaves at other cost levels, including the standard No-Cost setting. I study the within-subject relationship between P4's High-Cost and No-Cost strategies in these treatments by measuring each P4 subject's proximity to the Level-1 and Nash predictions at these two cost levels. An individual subject's proximity to a given theoretical prediction is measured using the Mean Absolute Deviation (MAD) from that prediction of their six reported strategies at that cost level. Table 5.3 presents a Markov transition matrix which tallies P4 subjects in BASE and ORDER by which of their MAD from the Nash and their MAD from the Level-1 prediction is smaller in High-Cost rounds (rows) and in No-Cost rounds (columns).

*Result 3.2: If Player 4's strategies are closer to Level-1 than Nash when the waiting cost is high, his strategies are more likely to be closer to Level-1 than Nash in the standard setting.*

Consistent with the bimodality of the distributions of P4 strategies, 47.6% of P4 subjects in BASE and ORDER use strategies closer to the Level-1 prediction than the Nash prediction in High-Cost rounds. This split of P4 subjects reveals an interesting correlation with their strategies in the standard herding game of No-Cost rounds. Of those whose High-Cost strategies are closer to Level-1 than Nash, 76.9% use strategies which are also closer to the Level-1 prediction than the Nash prediction in No-Cost rounds. According to McNemar's test, this relationship across cost levels is statistically significant ($p = .0135$). Hence, separating subjects by their behavior in a modification of a standard herding game, where Level-1 strategies are easily distinguishable from strategies of higher levels of thinking, allows me to predict which subjects are more likely to use strategies closer to the Level-1 than Nash in the standard setting, where the two types of behavior are much more difficult to distinguish.[26]

*Result 3.3: Differences in Player 4 strategies between when the the first two players' choices are independent and when they are correlated are consistent with Level-k thinking.*

The bimodality of P4 strategies in BASE is meaningful when compared to the distribution of P4 strategies in High-Cost rounds of 1-2-L1. The Level-1 strategy is 100 in High-Cost rounds of both 1-2-L1 and BASE, and consistently, the proportions of P4 strategies in [95,100] in these treatments (29.5% and 27.1%, respectively) are not significantly different ($p = 0.9731$). However, the strategy of Level-2 and higher in 1-2-L1 is to choose contrary to P3 for all but strong agreeing signals, while in BASE it is to follow P3 unconditionally. Consistently, only 9.4% of P4 strategies fall in [0,5] in High-Cost rounds of 1-2-L1, significantly less than the 24.8% observed in this interval in BASE ($p = 0.0078$). This difference between treatments indicates that while many P4 subjects behave

---

[26]Stahl and Wilson (1995) find some evidence that subjects' level of thinking is consistent across different games. In contrast, Georganas et al. (2012) find that level of thinking may or may not be consistent across similar games, and that subjects' level in one family of games may not be consistent with their level in another family of games.

consistently with Level-1, a substantial proportion use strategies which differ between treatments as predicted by higher levels of thinking.[27]

## 5.4 Analysis of ACT/SAT Scores

In this section, I test for a relationship between subjects' strategies and their cognitive ability, as measured by ACT and SAT scores. I obtained consent from 59.9% of subjects from BASE, ORDER and 1-2-L1 to access their ACT scores, SAT scores and major field of study through the Ohio State University registrar.[28] ACT scores were obtained for 45.9% of subjects from these treatments, while SAT scores were obtained and SAT-ACT concordance scores[29] used for another 14.0% of these subjects.[30]

As in Section 5.3, I use the Mean Absolute Deviation (MAD) of a subject's strategies from a given theoretical prediction to measure proximity to that prediction. Because MAD is essentially a fractional measure, I use the log-odds ratio of the MAD, $(log(\frac{MAD}{100-MAD}))$ as the dependent variable in these regressions to avoid predicted values outside the interval of possible strategies.[31] Using OLS, I regress this measure of proximity to a given theoretical prediction on indicators for whether a subject has an ACT or SAT-ACT concordance score in the top 5% of all test-takers or below the top 20% of all test-takers[32] and an indicator for having a quantitiative major, including math, science, engineering and economics. For each theoretical prediction, I conduct the regression at three levels of observation: using the MAD of a P4 subject's strategies from that prediction over (1) all cost levels for subjects in BASE, ORDER and 1-2-L1, (2) No-Cost rounds only for subjects in BASE and ORDER, and (3) High-Cost rounds only for subjects in BASE and ORDER. Table

---

[27]This result is consistent with findings of a p-beauty contest experiment by Coricelli and Nagel (2009). Subjects in this experiment whose strategies correspond to higher levels of thinking against human opponents tend to play a Level-1 strategy when matched with a randomizing computer, while subjects exhibiting lower levels of thinking behave similarly in both treatments.

[28]This is one of only a few studies in the experimental economics literature to use verified ACT or SAT scores (as opposed to self-reported scores) as a measure of cognitive ability. See Benjamin and Shapiro (2005), Casari et al. (2007), Ivanov et al. (2009, 2010) and Jones (2012) for other examples.

[29]See http://professionals.collegeboard.com/profdownload/act-sat-concordance-tables.pdf for SAT-ACT concordance tables.

[30]Summary statistics on these test scores are reported in Table C.2 in Appendix C.

[31]See Papke and Wooldridge (1996).

[32]ACT percentile is the appropriate measure because ACT scores are based on a rank-order scale and not an additive scale.

Table 5.4: OLS Regressions: Log-Odds Ratio of Player 4 Mean Deviation on Test Scores/Major

| Variable | Nash Estimate | (S.E.) | Level-1 Estimate | (S.E.) | Level-2 Estimate | (S.E.) |
|---|---|---|---|---|---|---|
| Mean deviation over all cost levels, BASE/ORDER/1-2-L1 | | | | | | |
| ACT in Top 5% | -0.290* | (0.173) | 0.438** | (0.214) | -0.237 | (0.172) |
| ACT below Top 20% | -0.222 | (0.182) | 0.144 | (0.225) | -0.223 | (0.182) |
| Quantitative Major | -0.180 | (0.215) | 0.183 | (0.266) | -0.235 | (0.214) |
| Constant | -0.347*** | (0.111) | -0.711*** | (0.137) | -0.426*** | (0.110) |
| Observations | 72 | | 72 | | 72 | |
| Mean deviation over No-Cost strategies only, BASE/ORDER | | | | | | |
| ACT in Top 5% | -0.574** | (0.280) | -0.274 | (0.275) | -0.463 | (0.289) |
| ACT below Top 20% | -0.387 | (0.347) | -0.251 | (0.339) | -0.519 | (0.363) |
| Quantitative Major | 0.006 | (0.357) | -0.137 | (0.350) | 0.134 | (0.381) |
| Constant | -0.263 | (0.177) | -0.758*** | (0.173) | -0.503*** | (0.183) |
| Observations | 51 | | 51 | | 50 | |
| Mean deviation over High-Cost strategies only, BASE/ORDER | | | | | | |
| ACT in Top 5% | -1.019** | (0.489) | 1.019** | (0.489) | -1.019** | (0.489) |
| ACT below Top 20% | -0.366 | (0.579) | 0.366 | (0.579) | -0.366 | (0.579) |
| Quantitative Major | -0.622 | (0.598) | 0.622 | (0.598) | -0.622 | (0.598) |
| Constant | 0.525* | (0.296) | -0.525* | (0.296) | 0.525* | (0.296) |
| Observations | 49 | | 49 | | 49 | |

5.4 reports the results of these regressions.

*Result 4: Player 4 subjects with an ACT score in the top 5% of all test-takers use strategies closer to the Nash prediction and farther from the Level-1 prediction.*

The regressions using the MAD over all cost levels for P4 subjects in BASE, ORDER and 1-2-L1 reveal evidence of a positive correlation between cognitive ability and proximity to the Nash prediction and a negative correlation between cognitive ability and proximity to the Level-1 prediction. Specifically, having an ACT or SAT-ACT concordance score in the top 5% of all test-takers makes the MAD from the Nash strategy significantly smaller (at the .1 level) and the MAD from the Level-1 strategy significantly larger (at the .05 level). This result suggests that a subject with high cognitive ability is more likely to learn through inference from P3's observed action and less likely to behave as if P3 chose randomly.[33]

The same regressions are also conducted for P4 strategies from BASE and ORDER only, separately for No-Cost and High-Cost rounds. Unlike the first set of regressions, the theoretical predictions used to calculate MAD do not vary across observations in these regressions. Consistent with results from the pooled data, I find that having an ACT or SAT-ACT concordance score in the top 5% of all test-takers makes the MAD from the Nash strategy significantly smaller (at the .05 level) in No-Cost rounds of BASE and ORDER. The effect on proximity to the Level-1 strategy is not significant in these rounds, but a weaker relationship with proximity to Level-1 is expected because the Level-1 strategy is at the midpoint of the strategy interval, which limits the magnitude of variation about this prediction.

In High-Cost rounds of BASE and ORDER, the maximum difference between the Nash and Level-1 strategies allows me to more easily differentiate between levels of thinking that motivate behavior. The regressions on P4 High-Cost strategies in these rounds reveal a clear relationship between test scores and proximity to the Nash and Level-1 predictions, suggesting that subjects with high cognitive ability use strategies significantly closer to the Nash prediction and farther from the Level-1 prediction (at the .05 level) where these two benchmarks are quite distinct. This result provides an explanation for the dichotomy of P4 behavior present in the data from these rounds.

Regressions using MAD from the Level-2 strategy (where it is different from Nash) as the dependent variable do not yield any significant results. Furthermore, having a score below the top 20% of all test-takers or a quantitative major does not significantly affect the proximity of P4 strategies to any of the three theoretical predictions. All of the above regression results are robust to the exclusion of test score or major from the equation, which does not change the significance of remaining coefficients.

By a strict interpretation of the theory, the Level-$k$ model does not apply to P3's problem in

---

[33]This result is consistent with the findings of Ivanov et al. (2009, 2010) that subjects in their endogenous-timing investment experiment with high SAT scores are more likely to respond as predicted to informational externalities. It is also consistent with the results of Burnham et al. (2009) and Gill and Prowse (2012), who find that subjects who guess lower in a p-beauty contest also perform better on tests of intelligence. In a p-beauty contest experiment with fMRI imaging by Coricelli and Nagel (2009), subjects with greater brain activity related to mental calculation use higher-level strategies. Camerer et al. (2004) also observe differences in level of thinking in p-beauty contests between subject pools of different abilities. In contrast, Georganas et al. (2012) find little evidence of a relationship between levels of thinking in other types of games and scores in several tests of cognitive ability.

BASE, ORDER and 1-2-L1 because she observes the choices of computer players with commonly known strategies, so there is no room for inconsistent beliefs about their rationality. However, I also study whether P3 subjects behave as if they hold incorrect beliefs about these computer players' strategies.[34] By this more liberal intepretation, the Level-$k$ benchmarks for P3 would be the same as those in 1-2-H (see Figure 3.4). I conduct the same regression on the pooled P3 data from all cost levels of BASE, ORDER and 1-2-L1 as is conducted for P4.[35] These regressions indicate that having an ACT score in the top 5% of all test-takers significantly reduces P3's MAD from the Nash and Level-1 strategies (at the .1 level). These effects are in the same direction because the Level-1 strategy is relatively close to the Nash strategy for P3. Having a score below the top 20% has no significant effect, but having a quantitative major significantly reduces a subject's MAD from Nash, Level-1 and Level-2 (at the .1, .01 and .1 levels, respectively). Because P3's payoffs and information are determined entirely by hers and the computer's decisions, her task is essentially a one-person decision problem. Hence, it makes sense that having a quantitative major, a proxy for the subject's numeracy and ability to read graphs, is as important if not more important than cognitive ability in determining her proximity to the Nash prediction.

# 6  Conclusion

This research provides insight into why people tend to deviate from Bayesian rationality in situations where it requires making inferences from the observed choices of others. Many people simply make no such inferences, behaving instead as if others choose randomly. On the other hand, a substantial proportion of people do gain information from observing others when they have sufficient confidence about the strategies others are following. When deviations occur, these findings suggest that those with high cognitive ability are less likely to be responsible.

There are many potential applications and directions for future research extending from these results, including financial markets and other contexts where inferences based on observed choices of others are critical to decision-making. The insights of this experiment can be applied more directly

---

[34]See Charness and Levin (2009) for an experiment in which Cursed play persists in one-person decision problems where beliefs about the rationality of others are not relevant.

[35]Results are reported in Table C.3 in Appendix C.

to network design and other problems where congestion is an important concern. In such contexts, results suggest that achieving the desired outcome should not hinge upon the assumption that people will sort themselves with common knowledge of rationality. Instead, many people should be expected to respond without higher-level reflection on the motives of others.

# References

[1] Anderson, L.R. (2001). "Payoff effects in information cascade experiments," *Economic Inquiry* 39, 609615.

[2] Anderson, L.R. and C.A. Holt. (1997). "Information Cascades in the Laboratory," *American Economic Review* 87(5), 847-862.

[3] Arthur, W.B. (1994). "Inductive Reasoning and Bounded Rationality," *American Economic Review Papers and Proceedings* 84(2), 406-411.

[4] Banerjee, A. (1992). "A simple model of herd behavior," *Quarterly Journal of Economics* 107(3), 797-818.

[5] Benjamin, D.J. and J.M. Shapiro. (2005). "Does Cognitive Ability Reduce Psychological Bias?" Working Paper.

[6] Bikhchandani, S., D. Hirshleifer and I. Welch. (1992). "A theory of fads, fashion, custom, and cultural change as information cascades," *Journal of Political Economy* 100(5), 992-1026.

[7] Brunner C. and J.K. Goeree. (2011). "The Wisdom of Crowds," Working Paper.

[8] Burnham, T., D. Cesarini, M. Johannesson, P. Lichtenstein and B. Wallace. (2009). "Higher cognitive ability is associated with lower entries in a p-beauty contest," *Journal of Economic Behavior and Organization* 72(1): 171-175.

[9] Camerer, C.F., T.-H. Ho and J.-K. Chong. (2004). "A Cognitive Hierarchy Model of Games," *Quarterly Journal of Economics* 119, 861-98.

[10] Casari, M., J.C. Ham and J.H. Kagel. (2007). "Selection Bias, Demographic Effects, and Ability Effects in Common Value Auction Experiments," *American Economic Review* 97(4), 1278-1304.

[11] Celen, B. and S. Kariv. (2004a). "Distinguishing informational cascades from herd behavior in the laboratory," *American Economic Review* 94, 484-497.

[12] Celen, B. and S. Kariv. (2004b). "Observational Learning Under Imperfect Information," *Games and Economic Behavior* 47, 72-86.

[13] Celen, B. and S. Kariv. (2005). "An Experimental Test of Observational Learning Under Imperfect Information," *Economic Theory* 26(3), 677-699.

[14] Celen, B., S. Kariv and A. Schotter. (2010). "An Experimental Test of Advice and Social Learning," *Management Science* 56(10), 1678-1701.

[15] Charness, G. and D. Levin. (2009). "The Origin of the Winner's Curse: A Laboratory Study," *American Economic Journal: Microeconomics* 1(1), 207-236.

[16] Coricelli, G. and R. Nagel. (2009). "Neural correlates of depth of strategic reasoning in medial prefrontal cortex," *Proceedings of the National Academy of the Sciences* 106(23): 9163-9168.

[17] Costa-Gomes, M., V.P. Crawford and B. Broseta. (2001). "Cognition and behavior in normal-form games: An experimental study," *Econometrica* 69(5): 1193-1235.

[18] Costa-Gomes, M. and V.P. Crawford. (2006). "Cognition and behavior in two-person guessing games: An experimental study," *American Economic Review* 96(5): 1737-1768.

[19] Crawford, V.P. and N. Iriberri. (2007). "Level-k auctions: Can a non-equilibrium model of strategic thinking explain the winner's curse and overbidding in private-value auctions?" *Econometrica* 75, 1721-1770.

[20] Dominitz, J. and A.A. Hung (2009). "Empirical models of discrete choice and belief updating in observational learning experiments," *Journal of Economic Behavior and Organization* 69, 94-109.

[21] Drehmann, M., J. Oechssler and A. Roider. (2007). "Herding with and without payoff externalities - an internet experiment," *International Journal of Industrial Organization* 25, 391-415.

[22] Eyster, E. and M. Rabin. (2005). "Cursed Equilibrium," *Econometrica* 73 1623-1672.

[23] Eyster, E. and M. Rabin. (2009). "Rational and Naive Herding," Working Paper.

[24] Eyster, E. and M. Rabin. (2010). "Naive Herding in Rich-Information Settings," *American Economic Journal: Microeconomics* 2 221-243.

[25] Fishbacher, U. (2007). "z-Tree: Zurich Toolbox for Ready-Made Economic Experiments," *Experimental Economics* 10, 171-178.

[26] Frey, M.C. and D.K. Detterman. (2004). "Scholastic assessment or $g$? The relationship between the SAT and general cognitive ability," *Psychological Science* 15(6), 373-378.

[27] Georganas, S., P.J. Healy and R.A. Weber. (2012). "On the Persistence of Strategic Sophistication," Working Paper.

[28] Gill, D. and V. Prowse. (2012). "Cognitive ability and learning to play equilibrium: A level-$k$ analysis," Working Paper.

[29] Goeree, J., T. Palfrey, B. Rogers and R. McKelvey. (2007). "Self-correcting Information Cascades," *Review of Economic Studies* 74: 733-762.

[30] Hung, A.A. and C.R. Plott (2001). "Information Cascades: Replication and an Extension to Majority Rule and Conformity-Rewarding Institutions," *American Economic Review* 91(5), 1508-1520.

[31] Jones, M.T. (2012). "Strategic Complexity and Cooperation: An Experimental Study," Working Paper.

[32] Koenig, K.A., M.C. Frey and D.K. Detterman. (2008). "ACT and general cognitive ability," *Intelligence* 36, 153-160.

[33] Kubler, D. and G. Weizsacker. (2004). "Limited depth of reasoning and failure of cascade formation in the laboratory," *Review of Economic Studies* 71, 425-441.

[34] Ivanov, A., D. Levin and J. Peck. (2009). "Hindsight, Foresight, and Insight: An Experimental Study of a Small-Market Investment Game with Common and Private Values," *American Economic Review* 99:4, 14841507.

[35] Ivanov, A., D. Levin and J. Peck. (2012). "Behavioral Biases in Endogenous-Timing Herding Games: An Experimental Study," *Journal of Economic Behavior and Organization* forthcoming.

[36] March, C., S. Krugel and A. Ziegelmeyer. (2012). "Do We Follow Private Information when We Should? Laboratory Evidence on Naive Herding," Working Paper.

[37] McKelvey, R. and T. Palfrey. (1995). "Quantal Response Equilibria in Normal Form Games," *Games and Economic Behavior* 10, 638.

[38] Nagel, R. (1995). "Unraveling in Guessing Games: An Experimental Study," *Review of Economic Studies* 85, 1313-26.

[39] Noth, M. and M. Weber. (2003). "Information Aggregation with Random Ordering: Cascades and Overconfidence," *Economic Journal* 113, 166-189.

[40] Owens, D. (2011). "An Experimental Study of Observational Learning with Payoff Externalities," Working Paper.

[41] Papke, L. and J.M. Wooldridge. (1996). "Econometric Methods for Fractional Response Variables with an Application to 401(k) Plan Participation Rates," *Journal of Applied Econometrics* 11, 619-632.

[42] Penczynski, S.P. (2012). "A level-$k$ model of social learning," Working Paper.

[43] Smith, L. and P. Sorensen. (2000). "Pathological Outcomes of Observational Learning," *Econometrica* 68(2), 371-398.

[44] Stahl, D.O. and P.O. Wilson. (1994). "Experimental Evidence on Players' Models of Other Players," *Journal of Economic Behavior and Organization* 25, 309-27.

[45] Stahl, D.O. and P.W. Wilson. (1995). "On players models of other players: Theory and experimental evidence," *Games and Economic Behavior* 10: 218-254.

[46] Veeraraghan, S. and L. D. Debo. (2008). "Is it Worth the Wait? Service Choice and Externalities When Waiting is Expensive," Working Paper.

[47] Weizsacker, G. (2010). "Do We Follow Others when We Should? A Simple Test of Rational Expectations," *American Economic Review* 100(5), 2340-2360.

[48] Ziegelmeyer, A., F. Koessler, J. Bracht and E. Winter. (2010). "Fragility of information cascades: an experimental study using elicited beliefs," *Experimental Economics* 13: 121-145.

# A    Derivation of Risk-Neutral Bayesian Nash Equilibrium

Suppose $x_{n-1} = R$. Risk-neutral player $n$ chooses alternative $R$ if and only if the following holds:

$$E[\frac{\sum_{i=1}^{4} \theta_i}{4} - C_n(x_1, ..., x_{n-1}, R)|\theta_n, x_{n-1} = R]$$
$$\geq E[1 - \frac{\sum_{i=1}^{4} \theta_i}{4} - C_n(x_1, ..., x_{n-1}, L)|\theta_n, x_{n-1} = R].$$

Because $\theta_{n+1}, ..., \theta_4$ are independent with mean $\frac{1}{2}$, this inequality can be re-written as,

$$E[\frac{\sum_{i=1}^{n-1} \theta_i + \theta_n + \frac{1}{2}(4-n)}{4} - C_n(x_1, ..., x_{n-1}, R)|\theta_n, x_{n-1} = R]$$
$$\geq E[1 - \frac{\sum_{i=1}^{n-1} \theta_i + \theta_n + \frac{1}{2}(4-n)}{4} - C_n(x_1, ..., x_{n-1}, L)|\theta_n, x_{n-1} = R],$$

which simplifies to:

$$\theta_n \geq \frac{n}{2} - E[\sum_{i=1}^{n-1} \theta_i - 2(C_n(x_1, ..., x_{n-1}, R) - C_n(x_1, ..., x_{n-1}, L))|x_{n-1} = R].$$

33

Hence, player $n$ uses a cutoff strategy given by:

$$x_n(x_{n-1} = R) = \begin{cases} R & \text{if } \theta_n \geq \hat{\theta}_n \\ L & \text{if } \theta_n < \hat{\theta}_n \end{cases},$$

where $\hat{\theta}_n = \frac{n}{2} - E[\sum_{i=1}^{n-1} \theta_i - 2(C_n(x_1, ..., x_{n-1}, R) - C_n(x_1, ..., x_{n-1}, L))|x_{n-1} = R]$. The problem is symmetric for $x_{n-1} = L$, so in this case the player follows a strategy given by:

$$x_n(x_{n-1} = L) = \begin{cases} R & \text{if } \theta_n \geq 1 - \hat{\theta}_n \\ L & \text{if } \theta_n < 1 - \hat{\theta}_n \end{cases}.$$

I now derive the Risk-Neutral Bayesian Nash Equilibrium strategies for Players 1 through 4.

Player 1: Because $\theta_2, \theta_3$ and $\theta_4$ are drawn independently and uniformly from $[0,1]$, it follows trivially that $\hat{\theta}_1 = \frac{1}{2}$ holds.

Player 2: Because neither option's capacity can be reached after only one player's choice, $E[\theta_1 - 2(C_2(x_1, R) - C_2(x_1, L))|x_1 = R] = E[\theta_1|x_1 = R] = \frac{3}{4}$ holds, which imples that $\hat{\theta}_2 = 1 - \frac{3}{4} = \frac{1}{4}$ holds.

Player 3: By Bayes' Rule it follows from $\hat{\theta}_1$ and $\hat{\theta}_2$ that $Pr(x_1 = R|x_2 = R) = \frac{3}{4}$ holds. Hence, $E[\theta_1 + \theta_2|x_2 = R] = \frac{3}{4}E[\theta_1 + \theta_2|x_1 = x_2 = R] + \frac{1}{4}E[\theta_1 + \theta_2|x_1 = L, x_2 = R] = \frac{3}{4}(\frac{5}{8} + \frac{6}{8}) + \frac{1}{4}(\frac{7}{8} + \frac{2}{8}) = \frac{21}{16}$ holds. Also, $E[2(C_3(x_1, R) - C_3(x_1, L))|x_2 = R] = 2\frac{3}{4}c = \frac{6c}{4}$ holds. Therefore, $\hat{\theta}_3$ is equal to the minimum of $\frac{3}{2} - \frac{21}{16} + \frac{6c}{4} = \frac{3+24c}{16}$ and 1 because $\frac{3+24c}{16} > 1$ implies that it is never optimal for Player 3 to follow Player 2. $\frac{3+24c}{16} > 1$ holds if and only if $c > \frac{13}{24}$ is satisfied.

Player 4: By Bayes' Rule it follows from $\hat{\theta}_1, \hat{\theta}_2$ and $\hat{\theta}_3$ that if $c \leq \frac{13}{24}$ is satisfied then $Pr(x_2 = R|x_3 = R) = \frac{13-24c}{16}$ holds. Hence, we have,

$$\begin{aligned} &E[\theta_1 + \theta_2 + \theta_3|x_3 = R] \\ &= \frac{13-24c}{16}(\frac{3}{4}E[\theta_1 + \theta_2 + \theta_3|x_1 = x_2 = x_3 = R] + \frac{1}{4}E[\theta_1 + \theta_2 + \theta_3|x_1 = L, x_2 = x_3 = R]) \\ &+ \frac{3+24c}{16}(\frac{1}{4}E[\theta_1 + \theta_2 + \theta_3|x_1 = x_3 = R, x_2 = L] + \frac{3}{4}E[\theta_1 + \theta_2 + \theta_3|x_1 = x_2 = L, x_3 = R]) \end{aligned},$$

where the following hold if $c \leq \frac{13}{24}$ is satisfied:

34

$$E[\theta_1 + \theta_2 + \theta_3 | x_1 = x_2 = x_3 = R] = \tfrac{5}{8} + \tfrac{6}{8} + \tfrac{19+24c}{32};$$

$$E[\theta_1 + \theta_2 + \theta_3 | x_1 = L, x_2 = x_3 = R] = \tfrac{7}{8} + \tfrac{2}{8} + \tfrac{19+24c}{32};$$

$$E[\theta_1 + \theta_2 + \theta_3 | x_1 = x_3 = R, x_2 = L] = \tfrac{1}{8} + \tfrac{6}{8} + \tfrac{29-24c}{32};$$

$$E[\theta_1 + \theta_2 + \theta_3 | x_1 = x_2 = L, x_3 = R] = \tfrac{3}{8} + \tfrac{2}{8} + \tfrac{29-24c}{32}.$$

Some algebra yields $E[\theta_1 + \theta_2 + \theta_3 | x_3 = R] = \frac{473 - 576c^2}{256}$. In addition, the following holds: $E[2(C_4(x_1, x_2, R) - C_4(x_1, x_2, L)) | x_3 = R] = 2(\frac{13-24c}{16}c + \frac{1}{4}\frac{3+24c}{16}c - \frac{3}{4}\frac{3+24c}{16}c) = \frac{368c - 1152c^2}{256}$. Therefore, if $c \leq \frac{13}{24}$ is satisfied then $\hat{\theta}_4 = 2 - \frac{473-576c^2}{256} + \frac{368c-1152c^2}{256} = \frac{39 + 368c - 576c^2}{256}$ holds. However, if $c > \frac{13}{24}$ is satisfied, then the following holds:

$$Pr(x_2 = R | x_3 = R) = 0;$$

$$E[\theta_1 + \theta_2 + \theta_3 | x_1 = x_3 = R, x_2 = L] = \tfrac{1}{8} + \tfrac{6}{8} + \tfrac{1}{2};$$

$$E[\theta_1 + \theta_2 + \theta_3 | x_1 = x_2 = L, x_3 = R] = \tfrac{3}{8} + \tfrac{2}{8} + \tfrac{1}{2}.$$

In this case, $E[\theta_1 + \theta_2 + \theta_3 | x_3 = R] = \frac{19}{16}$ and $E[2(C_4(x_1, x_2, R) - C_4(x_1, x_2, L)) | x_3 = R] = 2(\frac{1}{4}c - \frac{3}{4}c) = -c$ hold. Therefore, if $c > \frac{13}{24}$ is satisfied then $\hat{\theta}_4$ is equal to the maximum of $2 - \frac{19}{16} - c = \frac{13-16c}{16}$ and $0$ because $\frac{13-16c}{16} < 0$ implies that Player 4 should always follow Player 3. $\frac{13-16c}{16} < 0$ holds if and only if $c > \frac{13}{16}$ is satisfied.

Individual rationality is satisfied trivially for Players 1 and 2 because they never incur the waiting cost and for Player 3 because she can always avoid the cost by choosing contrary to Player 2. For Player 4, the individual rationality condition for choosing alternative $L$ given $x_3 = R$, $E[\frac{\sum_{i=1}^{4} \theta_i}{4} - C_4(x_1, x_2, x_3, R) | \theta_4, x_3 = R] \geq 0$, can be solved for the condition, $473 - 880c + 576c^2 \geq 0$, which holds for all $c \in [0, 1]$.

# B  Instructions and Screenshots

*Instructions for the BASE treatment are reprinted below. The instructions for 1-2-L1 are identical except for the graph depicting the strategies of computer Players 1 and 2. The ORDER and 1-2-H instructions use the same language as below with the necessary re-arranging and modifications.*

This is an experiment in the economics of decision making. If you follow these instructions carefully and make good decisions, you may earn a considerable amount of money which will be paid to you in cash at the end of the experiment.

The experiment is divided into 18 rounds. At the beginning of the experiment, you will be randomly assigned a role of either Player 3 or Player 4, and you will keep the same role in every round of the experiment. At the beginning of each round, you will be matched randomly and anonymously with a player of the other role, creating a match between Player 3 and Player 4. The match in each round is determined independently of matches in previous rounds. You and the person with whom you are matched will each make a choice after choices are made by two computer players, Player 1 and Player 2.

Each player is asked to choose one of two alternatives, LEFT and RIGHT. Choices are made in sequence: computer Player 1 chooses first, then computer Player 2, followed by human Player 3 and finally human Player 4.

Each player receives a private signal, which is a number drawn randomly and uniformly from the interval [0,100], independent of the private signals drawn for the other players. That is, for each player, each number in the interval [0,100] is equally likely to be drawn as that players private signal, regardless of which numbers are drawn for the other players. All players see only their own signal and do not see the signals of any other players.

Players 2, 3 and 4 see the choice of the player who chooses immediately before they do, but not the choices of the other players. That is, Player 2 sees the choice of Player 1, Player 3 sees the choice of Player 2, and Player 4 sees the choice of Player 3. Players see the choice of the preceding player (LEFT or RIGHT), but not the private signal of the preceding player.

When it is your turn to make a choice, you will see the choice of the preceding player (LEFT or RIGHT) on your computer screen, and you will be asked to enter a critical number between 0 and 100 before your private signal is shown to you. If your private signal turns out to be LESS than this number, your choice will be LEFT, and if your private signal turns out to be GREATER than this number, your choice will be RIGHT. In other words, when you enter this critical number, it means that for each possible private signal greater than this number, you would choose RIGHT, and for each possible private signal less than this number, you would choose LEFT. After you enter this number, your private signal will be drawn and your choice will be made for you according to the number you enter. When the round ends, your private signal will be shown to you along with your chosen alternative.

Payoffs for this experiment are denominated in Experimental Currency Units (ECUs). Your net payoff in ECUs in a given round is equal to the gross value of your chosen alternative minus any cost you incur.

The gross value of RIGHT in a given round is equal to the average of the private signals drawn for all four players in that round. The gross value of LEFT is equal to 100 minus the average of the private signals drawn for all four players in that round. For example, if the four private signals drawn are 11, 42, 83 and 20 then the average of the signals is $(11 + 42 + 83 + 20)/4$, which is equal to 39. Hence, the gross value of RIGHT is 39 ECUs and the gross value of LEFT is 61 ECUs $(100 - 39 = 61)$ in that round.

Players 3 and 4 incur a cost if they choose the same alternative as at least two of the preceding players. The cost in each round will be equal to 0, 35 or 85, and the cost is the same for both Players 3 and 4 in any given round. For example, suppose the cost is 35. If both Players 1 and 2 chose the same alternative as Player 3 in that round then 35 ECUs are subtracted from the gross value of Player 3's chosen alternative to determine her net payoff for the round. Otherwise, Player 3 does not pay the cost. If at least two of Players 1, 2 and 3 chose the same alternative as Player 4 in that round, 35 ECUs are subtracted from the gross value of Player 4s chosen alternative to determine her net payoff for the round. Otherwise, Player 4 does not pay the cost. Players 1 and 2 never incur a cost.

The computer players, Player 1 and Player 2, are programmed to choose according to the rules shown in the graph below, which includes Player 1s private signal on the horizontal axis and Player 2s private signal on the vertical axis. The solid line inside the graph represents the rule followed by computer Player 1. If it receives a private signal to the right of this line, it chooses RIGHT, and if it receives a private signal to the left of this line, it chooses LEFT. The dotted line inside the graph represents the rule followed by computer Player 2. If it receives a signal above this line, it chooses

RIGHT, and if it receives a signal below this line, it chooses LEFT. The regions of the graph are labeled by the choices Players 1 and 2 make for each pair of Player 1 and Player 2 signals in that region.

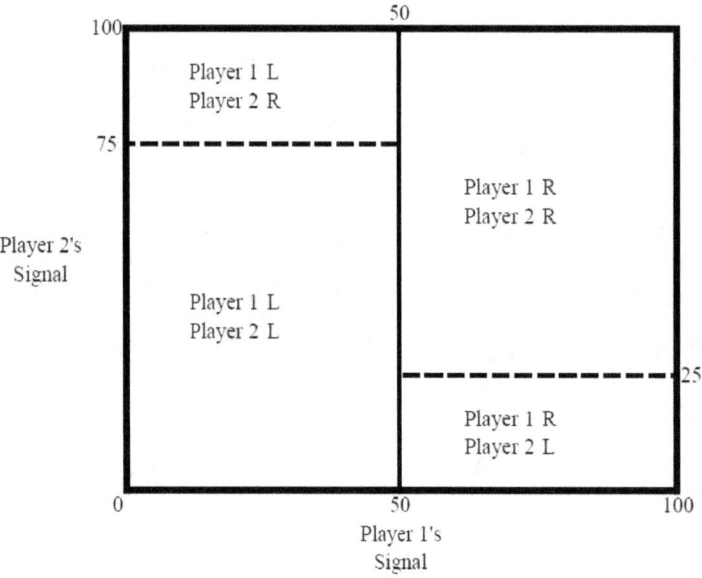

The cost will be 0, 35 and 85 for six rounds each and will be known (and the same) for both players, but the order in which these 18 rounds will be played is determined randomly. For each of the three cost levels, one of the six rounds played at that cost will be drawn randomly. You will be paid your earnings for only these three rounds. Because you do not know which rounds will be chosen for payment, you should play each round as if you will be paid for it. At the end of the experiment, you will be paid $0.10 per ECU earned in the three rounds selected for payment plus the starting balance of 50 ECUs. You will also receive the participation fee of $5.

Before we begin, we will play two trial rounds that do not count for payment so that you can get familiar with the software. Your role in the trial rounds (Player 3 or Player 4) will be the same as in the rest of the experiment. If you have any questions about the instructions, please ask them now. If you have questions during the experiment, please raise your hand and one of the experimenters will assist you. Please turn off your cell phones at this point. You should not communicate with any of the other participants for the duration of the experiment.

Figure B.1: Choice Screen

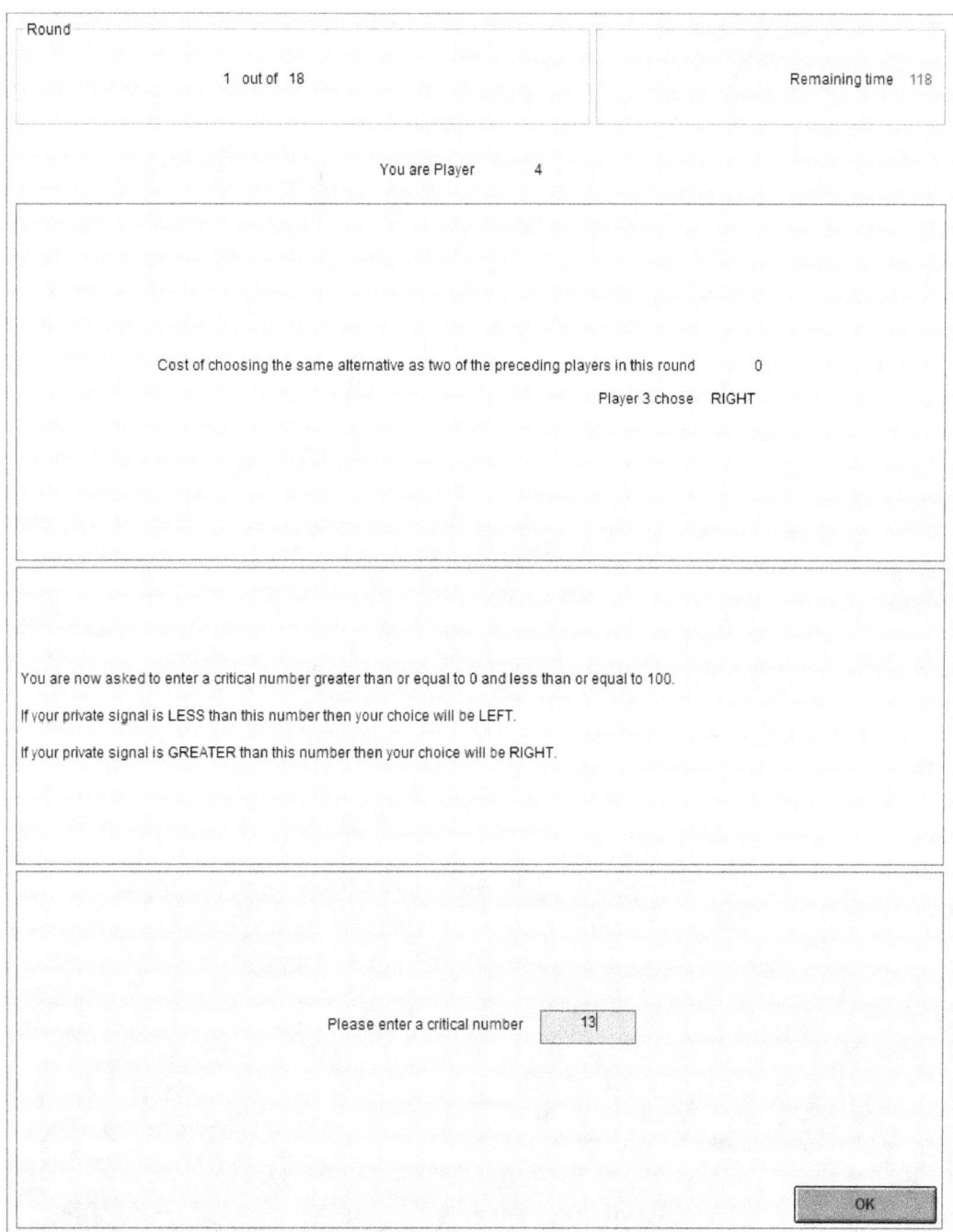

Figure B.2: Feedback Screen

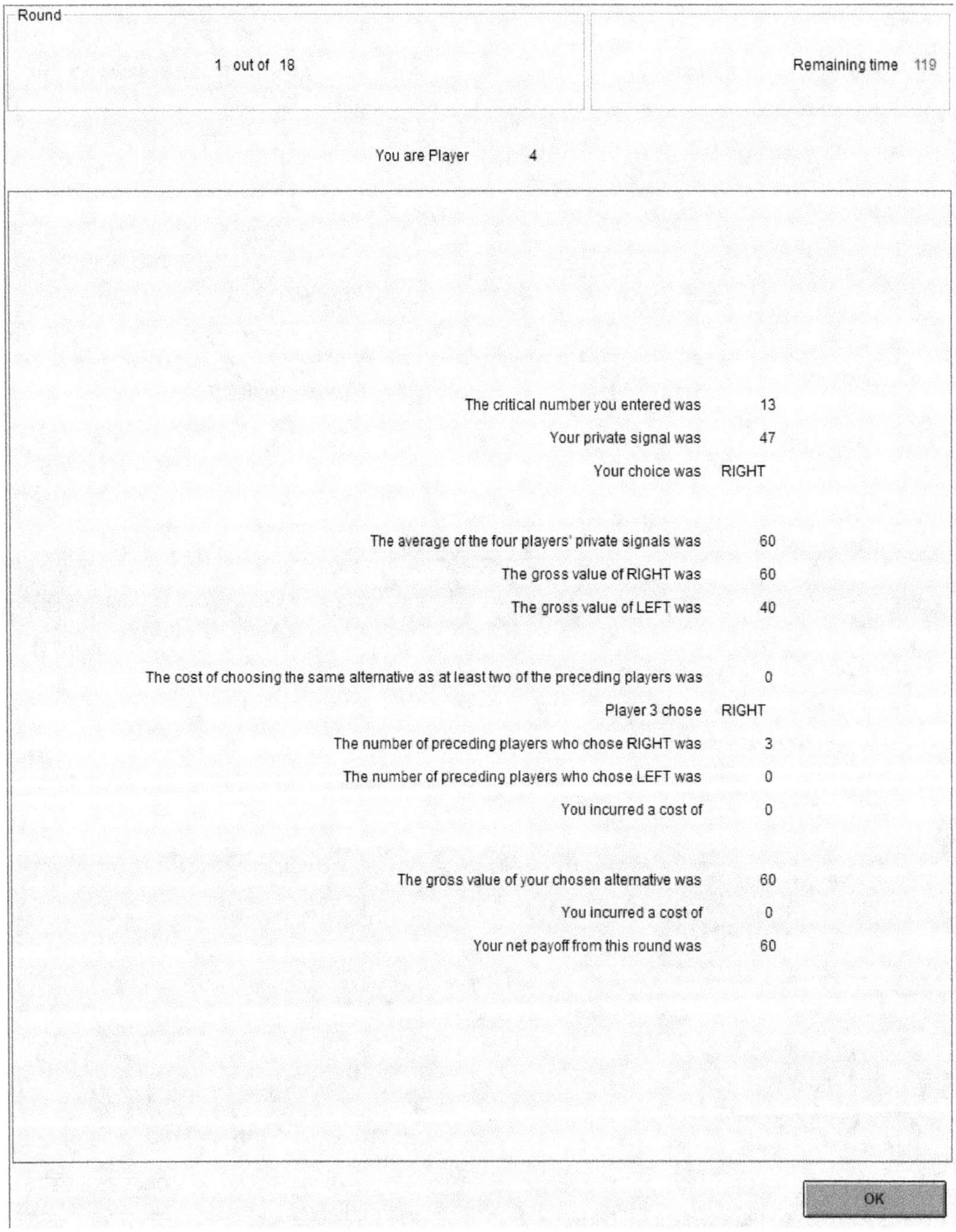

| Round | |
|---|---|
| 1 out of 18 | Remaining time 119 |

You are Player 4

The critical number you entered was 13
Your private signal was 47
Your choice was RIGHT

The average of the four players' private signals was 60
The gross value of RIGHT was 60
The gross value of LEFT was 40

The cost of choosing the same alternative as at least two of the preceding players was 0
Player 3 chose RIGHT
The number of preceding players who chose RIGHT was 3
The number of preceding players who chose LEFT was 0
You incurred a cost of 0

The gross value of your chosen alternative was 60
You incurred a cost of 0
Your net payoff from this round was 60

OK

# C   Figures and Tables

Figure C.1: Player 3 Strategies by Player 2 Choice

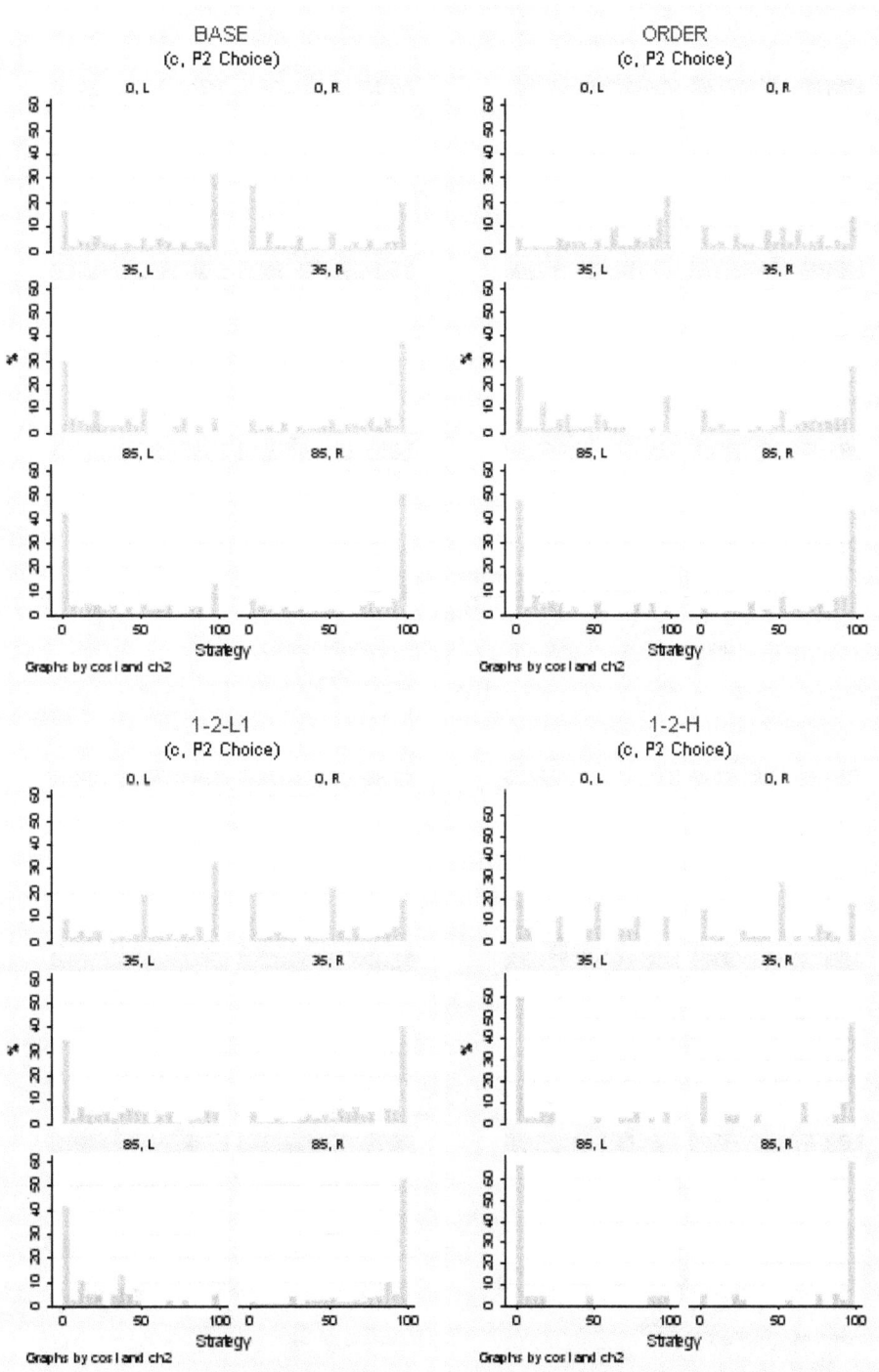

Figure C.2: Player 4 Strategies by Player 3 Choice

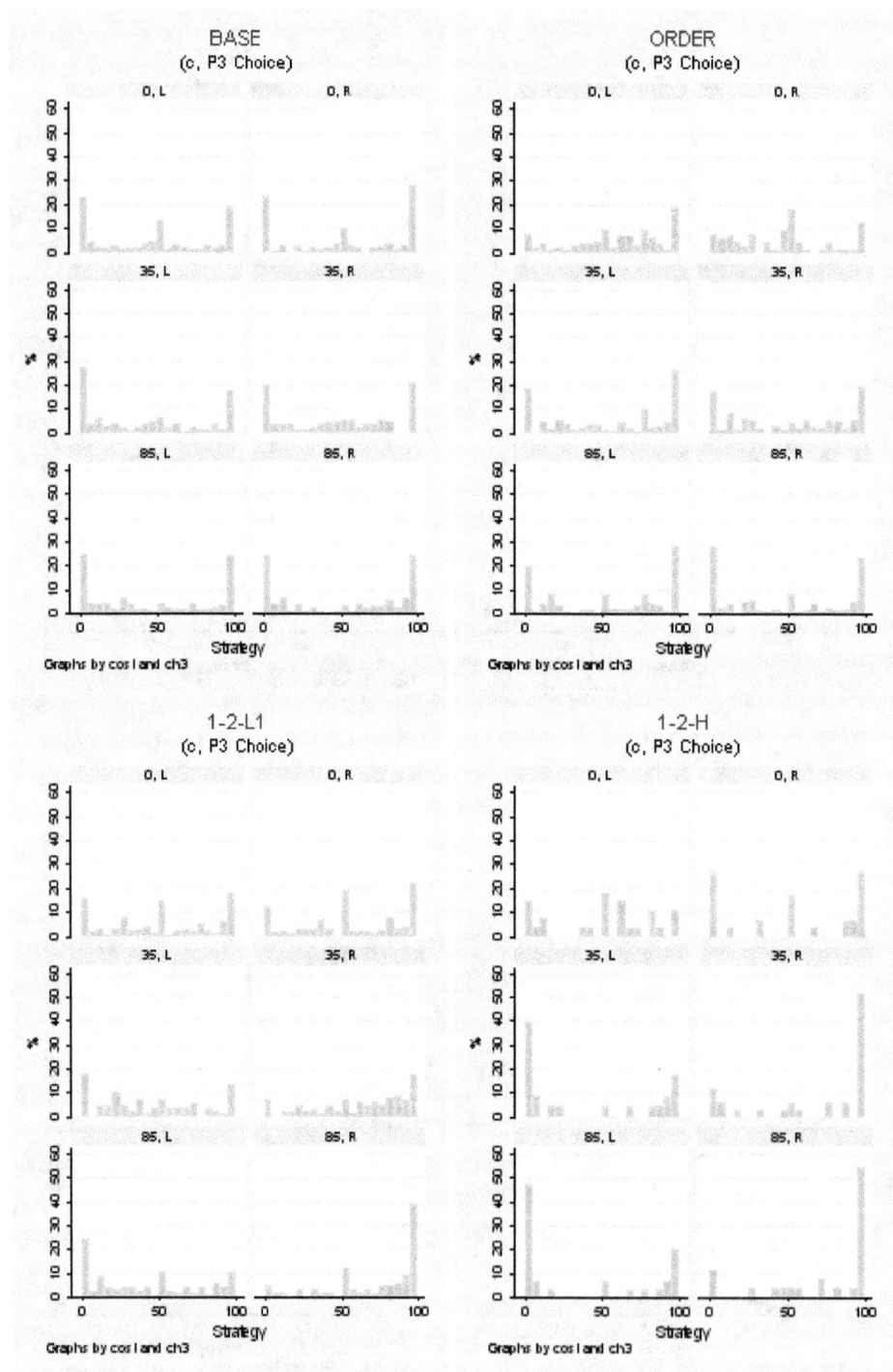

Figure C.3: Player 1 and Player 2 Strategies in 1-2-H

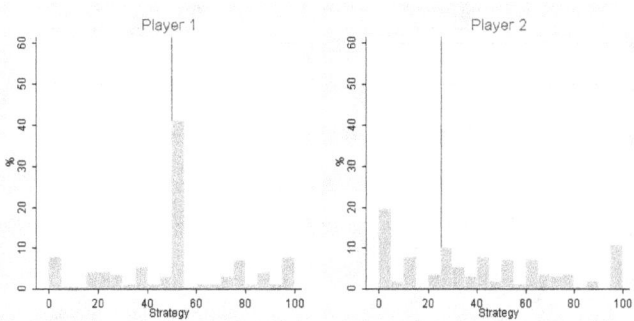

Table C.1: Mean Strategies, First and Last Round at Each Cost Level

| Treatment | Setting | Player 3 | | | Player 4 | | |
|---|---|---|---|---|---|---|---|
| | | Nash | First | Last | Nash | First | Last |
| BASE | No-Cost | 19 | 49.0 | 37.5 | 15 | 58.7 | 51.0 |
| | Low-Cost | 71 | 67.6 | 73.5 | 39 | 61.2 | 50.6 |
| | High-Cost | 100 | 60.9 | 78.6 | 0 | 53.5 | 50.1 |
| ORDER | No-Cost | 19 | 54.6 | 45.6 | 15 | 42.3 | 46.3 |
| | Low-Cost | 71 | 61.1 | 56.5 | 39 | 48.5 | 49.1 |
| | High-Cost | 100 | 67.1 | 82.1 | 0 | 54.9 | 46.6 |
| 1-2-L1 | No-Cost | 25 | 52.5 | 46.8 | 19 | 50.6 | 53.7 |
| | Low-Cost | 60 | 61.5 | 77.1 | 59 | 56.7 | 63.3 |
| | High-Cost | 100 | 76.2 | 80.0 | 75 | 59.3 | 66.6 |
| 1-2-H | No-Cost | 19 | 63.9 | 47.6 | 15 | 61.8 | 48.7 |
| | Low-Cost | 71 | 66.0 | 91.0 | 39 | 59.2 | 58.2 |
| | High-Cost | 100 | 67.4 | 87.7 | 0 | 81.9 | 54.9 |

Table C.2: ACT and SAT-ACT Concordance Score Summary Statistics

| Median | 27 |
|---|---|
| Mean | 27.58 |
| Std. Err. | 0.289 |
| % of BASE/ORDER/1-2-L1 Subjects' Scores Obtained* | 59.9% |
| % with ACT | 45.9% |
| % with SAT Only** | 14.0% |
| % with Score in Top 5% | 15.3% |
| % with Score below Top 20% | 14.0% |

*64.0% of BASE, 62.8% of ORDER and 52.6% of 1-2-L1 subjects.

**SAT-ACT concordance scores used.

43

Table C.3: OLS Regressions: Log-Odds Ratio of Player 3 Mean Deviation on Test Scores/Major

| Variable | Nash | | Level-1 | | Level-2 | |
|---|---|---|---|---|---|---|
| | Estimate | (S.E.) | Estimate | (S.E.) | Estimate | (S.E.) |
| Mean deviation over all cost levels, BASE/ORDER/1-2-L1 | | | | | | |
| ACT Score in Top 5% | -0.246* | (0.139) | -0.309* | (0.162) | -0.213 | (0.135) |
| ACT Score below Top 20% | 0.072 | (0.144) | 0.106 | (0.168) | 0.035 | (0.139) |
| Quantitative Major | -0.315* | (0.158) | -0.605*** | (0.185) | -0.296* | (0.153) |
| Constant | -0.772*** | (0.094) | -0.825*** | (0.109) | -0.788*** | (0.091) |
| Observations | 73 | | 73 | | 73 | |

# D  Risk Aversion

In this Appendix, I explore the impact of risk-aversion on the Bayesian Nash equilibrium by solving numerically for the equilibrium strategies of Players 3 and 4 under the assumption that the utility of choice $x_n$ is given by $U(x_n) = \sqrt{\pi(x_n)}$, where $\pi(x_n)$ is the payoff of choice $x_n$ and all players $1, .., n-1$ are assumed to behave according to the risk-neutral Nash. These strategies are denoted by $\hat{\theta}_3^{RA}$ and $\hat{\theta}_4^{RA}$ and shown below along with their risk-neutral alternatives ($\hat{\theta}_3^{RN}$ and $\hat{\theta}_4^{RN}$) below:

$$\hat{\theta}_3^{RA} \approx \begin{cases} .1873 & \text{if } c = 0 \\ .7316 & \text{if } c = .35 \\ 1 & \text{if } c = .85 \end{cases} \qquad \hat{\theta}_4^{RA} \approx \begin{cases} .1520 & \text{if } c = 0 \\ .3865 & \text{if } c = .35 \\ .1780 & \text{if } c = .85 \end{cases}$$

$$\hat{\theta}_3^{RN} = \begin{cases} .1875 & \text{if } c = 0 \\ .7125 & \text{if } c = .35 \\ 1 & \text{if } c = .85 \end{cases} \qquad \hat{\theta}_4^{RN} \approx \begin{cases} .1523 & \text{if } c = 0 \\ .3798 & \text{if } c = .35 \\ 0 & \text{if } c = .85 \end{cases}$$

These risk-averse strategies bear negligible differences from the risk-neutral strategies with one exception: the equilibrium strategy for a risk-averse P4 with $c = .85$ chooses contrary to P3 for a substantial range of strong disagreeing signals, whereas the risk-neutral strategy is to follow P3 unconditional on his private signal. Hence, if risk aversion plays an important role in the experiment, it should express itself in deviations from the Nash only for P4 at a high waiting cost.

44

# E  Subjects Satisfying Basic Rationality

Table E.1: Effects of Treatment and Cost Level for Subjects Satisfying Basic Rationality

| BASE/ORDER Prediction | | No-Cost | Low-Cost | High-Cost | 1-2-L1 Prediction | | No-Cost | Low-Cost | High-Cost |
|---|---|---|---|---|---|---|---|---|---|
| Nash | P3 | 19 | 71 | 100 | Nash | P3 | 25 | 60 | 100 |
|  | P4 | 15 | 38 | 0 |  | P4 | 19 | 59 | 75 |
| Level-2 | P4 | 25 | 40 | 0 | Level-2 | P4 | 25 | 65 | 75 |
| Level-1 | P4 | 50 | 85 | 100 | Level-1 | P4 | 50 | 85 | 100 |
| Mean Strategy | | No-Cost | Low-Cost | High-Cost | Mean Strategy | | No-Cost | Low-Cost | High-Cost |
| BASE | P3 | 26.8 <<< | 68.7 | 74.1 | 1-2-L1 | P3 | 28.3 <<< | 74.8 <<< | 86.9 |
|  | P4 | 35.3 | 33.2 | 37.4 |  | P4 | 40.1 <<< | 54.8** << | 65.4*** |
| ORDER | P3 | 33.5 <<< | 64.4 << | 81.2 | 1-2-H$^†$ | P3 | 36.8 | 61.0 | 79.2 |
|  | P4 | 33.4 < | 44.7 | 44.0 |  | P4 | 38.8 << | 69.7*** | 63.8* |

Between-cost-level difference significant at: <<< .01 level, << .05 level, < .1 level.

Between-treatment difference (compared to BASE) significant at: *** .01 level, ** .05 level, * .1 level.

$^†$1-2-H: Nash same as BASE/ORDER; Level-2 same as P3 Nash/P4 Level-2 in 1-2-L1; Level-1 same as P4 Level-1s.

In this Appendix, I study the behavior of subjects whose mean No-Cost strategy satisfies basic rationality in the sense that it does not choose contrary to the immediate predecessor given an agreeing signal (i.e., the mean No-Cost strategy is less than or equal to 50). The percentages of subjects satisfying basic rationality in BASE, ORDER, 1-2-L1 and 1-2-H, respectively, are 58.1%, 59.0%, 59.0% and 50.0% for P3 and 39.5%, 74.4%, 41.0% and 57.1% for P4.[36] Table E.1 reports these subjects' mean strategies by treatment and cost level.

Differences in mean P3 strategies between cost levels are qualitatively similar to the results obtained from the full data, but larger in magnitude. For P4, Low-Cost strategies differ significantly from No-Cost strategies as predicted in ORDER, 1-2-L1 and 1-2-H, although the effect remains insignificant in BASE. P4's mean High-Cost and Low-Cost strategies in 1-2-L1 also differ significantly as predicted by the Nash equilibrium. I find that P4's mean High- and Low-Cost strategies differ significantly between the 1-2-L1 and BASE treatments such that following P3 is less likely in 1-2-L1, as predicted by the Nash. These findings suggest that subjects who satisfy a basic rationality condition in rounds with no waiting cost generally respond to the capacity constraint and waiting cost as predicted by Nash equilibrium.

In an effort to explain what determines whether subjects satisfy basic rationality, I investigate

---

[36]For comparison, Celen and Kariv (2005) report that 60.8% of strategies in their experiment satisfy the same basic rationality condition.

Table E.2: Probits Reporting Marginal Effects of Test Scores/Major on Basic Rationality

| Variable | Player 3 Estimate | (S.E.) | Player 4 Estimate | (S.E.) |
|---|---|---|---|---|
| Score in Top 5% | 0.247 | (0.143) | 0.270* | (0.134) |
| Score below Top 20% | 0.080 | (0.138) | -0.031 | (0.144) |
| Quantitative Major | -0.029 | (0.163) | 0.118 | (0.169) |
| Observations | 73 | | 72 | |

the relationships between subjects' academic records and the proximity of their strategies to the theoretical predictions. Table E.2 reports the results of probit regressions with a dependent variable taking 1 as its value if a subject satisfies basic rationality and 0 otherwise. Explanatory variables include indicators for whether a subject has an ACT or SAT-ACT concordance score in the top 5% of all test-takers or below the top 20% of all test-takers and an indicator for having a quantitiative major.

For P4, having a test score in the top 5% of all test-takers is estimated to raise the probability of basic rationality by 27 percentage points (significant at the .1 level).[37] The marginal significance of this estimate combined with its large magnitude suggest that the likelihood of satisfying basic rationality in rounds with no waiting cost is correlated with cognitive ability for P4. For P3, I find no significant relationship between cognitive ability and basic rationality, though the magnitude of the estimate (24.7 percentage points) is similarly large.

---

[37]Probit regressions using only test scores or only major as explanatory variables do not yield important differences from the results of the regressions including all of the explanatory variables presented in Table E.2.

www.ingramcontent.com/pod-product-compliance
Lightning Source LLC
Chambersburg PA
CBHW081235170526
45165CB00009B/3060